YOUR CHILD IS YOUR GUIDE

*ACTIVATE THE REMEMBRANCE
OF THE DIVINE BOND BETWEEN
YOU AND YOUR CHILD*

MICHELLE BOWEN

YOUR CHILD IS YOUR GUIDE

Copyright © 2020 by Michelle A. Bowen

Edited by Maria A. Reid, Cover Design by Damonza.com

FOR YOU READING THIS RIGHT NOW.
MAY WE CONTINUE TO HAVE FUN
EXPERIENCING THAT IT IS SAFE TO
FOLLOW OUR HEARTS IN PARENTHOOD
AND IN GENERAL.

TABLE OF CONTENTS

I AM sovereign

I AM love

PRACTICE #4

The Smile Method

I AM waking up

I AM not a bully

I AM respectful

I AM worthy

I AM devoted

WE ARE one

PRACTICE #5

The Call-Out Method

I AM infinite

I AM trusting my self

I AM free

I AM aware

I AM confident

I AM making the higher choice

PRACTICE #6

The You-Are-Invited-to-The-Party Method

I AM authentic

I AM home

I AM taking my power back

I AM unconquerable

I AM here to play

I AM unconditional love incarnate

MICHELLE BOWEN

YOUR CHILD IS YOUR GUIDE

EVERYTHING IN THE PAST HAS MADE US WHO WE ARE NOW, WHICH ARE BEINGS WHO WANT TO OPERATE DIFFERENTLY AS PARENTS THAN WE HAVE BEEN CONDITIONED TO. THIS DESIRE IN US, THAT OUR PROGRAMMING HAS INSPIRED, IS A BLESSING TO THE GENERATIONS THAT COME FORTH AFTER US.

SO WE THANK THE PAST.

WE THANK OUR PARENTS.

WE THANK EVERYTHING THAT WE NEVER IMAGINED WE WOULD BE BOTH FORGIVING OF AND THANKFUL FOR.

TO HARBOR JUDGEMENT AND VENGEANCE TOWARDS THOSE WHO PLAYED A ROLE IN OUR PROGRAMMING LIMITS OUR CAPACITY TO ACTUALIZE OUR LIMITLESSNESS AND MAKES IT ABOUT US.

THIS ISN'T ABOUT US.

To receive the greatest benefit from this book, I invite you to practice the *Breathe It Out and Smile* method when interacting with your children during the time that you are reading this book.

It is simple.

When you feel any resistance at all, breathe deeply until it passes before reacting.

And then, smile. Even if it does not seem like a real smile. Allow your lips to form a smile after you have taken some deep breaths.

Example: Your child breaks something in the living room and you feel the anger, frustration, or any resistance start to arise within you. With this practice, you immediately start to breathe deeply. You continue to breathe deeply until you notice that the heavy emotions have passed. Then smile. You do not have to keep the smile on your face. What matters is the action itself for even just a moment.

You then go into the living room and respond to your child after.

This practice can be applied in addition to any of the other practices provided in this book.

The potency of the practice is in the application.

The more you apply the practices, the more you see the magic of doing so.

I AM being divinely guided

Currently, your child is your teacher. If the curriculum between you and your child was not so deeply rooted in unconditional love, I would say you could grade yourself based on how you are responding to your child; but, there is no grading scale in this particular school of love between parent and child. There is only awareness of where you are and where you want to be in relation to your child and becoming that version by taking actions that are representative of that higher version of you. By the end of this book, the teacher will become the student. You and your child will forever learn from one another; however, by the end of this book, your developing child will be able to see their future through you. Embodiment. True maturity. The child will be able to witness embodiment via their caretakers; therefore, they will be able to see and experience unconditional love, abundance, freedom, sovereignty, problem-solving skills, emotional maturity, awareness, and flow through an adult thus showing them what they are capable of. I cannot guarantee that they will witness the embodiment of a higher version of yourself because I will teach you how to be sovereign, abundant, and unconditionally loving, but instead I can guarantee that because unconditional love, sovereignty, and more are what is both remembered and amplified as you put your relationship with your child first. Ultimately, it is yourself that you will be putting first but you will be doing so by prioritizing your awareness regarding your relationship with your child. I say unconditional love, sovereignty, and more is remembered because they could never be something new to you as they are what you naturally are.

Over time since your birth, your sovereignty and sense of unity has been stifled by conditioning. It is worth noting that, for most of us, our parents were operating from a place of needing to see something to believe it. Needing to see something transpire in the physical to smile and be thankful. Needing to get the raise at work first and then be grateful. Needing to get the partner first and then feel a sense of worth. Needing the child to behave first and then cuddle them. Needing all bills to be paid first to feel secure. This is what a lot of us witnessed and, make no mistake, it was impressed upon our subconscious minds. This makes it easy for the behavior we witnessed as a child to be our default mode; even the behaviors we witnessed and experienced that we did not like.

As you make the decision in each moment to be the parent you want to be instead of the parent you have been conditioned to be, unconditional love, sovereignty, emotional maturity, awareness, and flow are the byproducts of that decision. Every being is on the path to embodying the full magnitude of their true nature in physical form. Whether they will in this lifetime or not is not for me to know. However, if any child's parent is reading this book, I do know that witnessing a parent embodied as their true self will aid in their own embodiment and greatly impact their childhood and the years following.

Once you gain some space between the thoughts and emotions to which you have identified over the years, and are more clear that you are not what is transient but are instead what allows for what is transient in nature to occur, you are then able to reside as what you truly are and, even better, you can bring the love that you really are into your relationship with your child and come from that space while interacting with your child, instead of reacting based on conditioning.

One does not have to deep dive into the physics or mechanics of it all to realize who you are at your core. There are thousands of books on self-realization and there is nothing at all wrong with reading them to dive deeper; however, you can also embody right now in this moment who you know to be the version of you that feels amazing and is more reflective of who you are at your core by responding with love and compassion to your child's request for something different than what you gave her for lunch. Or by responding to your child's tantrum in a way that you, as that child, would love to be responded to, with comfort and understanding.

You are given hundreds of opportunities throughout the day through interactions with your child to anchor the qualities that you want to flow continuously in your life. How you respond to life is how life responds to you. You are constantly giving to life the energy that you are calling forth back to you. Your child is no exception, although most of us have been raised as though they are. This is not so. Thinking that our children are the exception to this energetic exchange is what keeps us bound to our conditioning, and causes resentment towards our children because we tend to think they are the cause of our suffering. They are not.

We have been conditioned to believe that we must control our children and treat them less than we would treat an adult in many ways. Treating them in that way fuels separation consciousness and causes friction between parent and child. This is the old way of doing things, in general, for our species. We are moving beyond separation, so how we parent is also morphing into a more unified way of parenting. When we truly look at how we react to our children we can see that we act from fear.

Logically, it does not seem as though it makes sense that we fear our children; but anytime we treat anyone outside of us as though they are separate from us there is no ability to love. If someone or something is apart from us then it can hurt us. If it is seen as part of us then we do not go into a state of fear. Our fear of our children over the years looks like reacting by way of yelling, spanking, treating them as less than, etc. Our minds will justify this way of parenting because it keeps us safe. We feel threatened in those moments that we react. In order to survive, we react in the ways that we do instead of responding with love. We do this because we have been conditioned to. This is what we experienced and witnessed as children. However, it is not effective, and it does not feel good.

What I realized when I had my child and was committed to not using physical discipline was that when we change our tone alone, without the use of physical discipline, it has the same impact as if we had struck them. How is this possible? Because it is all about energy. Our children feel us more than they hear us, and when we spank them it only compounds the issue at hand. It sends the message that if people do not listen to us, then we have the right to hit them.

So, for my child, I had to realize that yelling and even the harsh tones were violent to a degree, but felt much better than spanking her. It was a process for me, especially with the understanding I had about my energy and resistance. I had to overcome a lot of guilt and shame for the reactions that I had with my daughter, even after years of seeking and consuming information that resonated with me on a deep level regarding who I am at my core. I beat myself up a lot because I was not accepting where I was, and was instead blaming parenthood for causing me to step out of my true nature; and to act in ways I knew were not in alignment with who I was. I did not know that when I accepted where I was, I would see the opportunity that being a parent provided regarding accelerating on my path and being the love that I knew myself to be. I thought I was done healing and did not know that I had only just begun.

We are thanking the old way of parenting for showing us what has not been working for quite some time and what we do not prefer; and embarking on an unconditionally loving-based approach that will impact future generations. Your grandchildren and great-grandchildren are grateful beyond measure for the work that you are doing. I say work because every attempt to override conditioned behavior is work. The rewards are most fulfilling and have a serious impact on the planet.

PRACTICE #1

The Change-of-Tone Method

With this practice, you will make it a point to speak to your child in a softer tone than usual. To see very obvious results, I would do it for a week minimum. You will see a difference in how your child receives anything you say which will result in a different manifestation of their own response and a leveling up of your relationship. Practiced enough, you will start to notice your tone in your own self talk soften.

So often, we talk to our children the way we talk to ourselves, which is not always the most loving. Focusing on actually saying loving words moment to moment may seem a bit taxing in practice and not always authentic. Practicing a softening of the tone of your voice can greatly impact you and others vibrationally; and it is not causing you to change the words themselves, but instead your tone alone. Try it. Witness your child's delight in the difference.

I AM able

I am not here because I am an expert on parenting. I am here because my daughter showed me how I was still a slave to my conditioning. Prior to my daughter's conception, I was reading Eckhart Tolle and was learning increasingly about consciousness. I had only just jumped down the rabbit hole. I was just starting to read and listen to more of Adyashanti, Paramahansa Yogananda, and a few others' work at the time. I was genuinely asking God for more patience and often expressing a desire to feel love, gratitude, and joy deeply. I had started to speak more to God while on the way to work in the mornings, before the work of the before-mentioned writers entered my awareness. I did not know at the time that the love I yearned to feel deeply was already natural for me to feel in abundance, and that there were conditioned ways of thinking and reacting to the world that interrupted the flow. I was given what I was asking for in the form of a child. A child who, while caring for her, would allow me opportunities to either continue creating a life without connecting to the flow of that love, or start creating a life in the flow of the love that is always here in each moment. Conditioned ways of doing, thinking, and being were the only things in the way of everything I ever wanted and much more.

You want love? Be love. The times where it is hard to be love are the times that are calling for reflection. Becoming a parent allowed for a lot of reflection in instances where I was not being what I preferred to be in the moment. There was a lot of reflection and course correction. Before the reflection and course correcting, I first had to look at where I truly was and see that it was not who I wanted to continue becoming. Taking an especially deep look at myself where I was did not come until years after consuming a lot of information on doing just that very thing. I got to a point where I was fed up with living a loop of reactionary behaviors with the same consequences.

For the first few years of my awakening and seeking self-realization, I separated my daughter from the process. My journey started a few years before she was born; but after her birth, I just did not group her with the rest of the population that I had to apply the teachings with. It was all uncharted territory; but parenthood was extremely new and very much in my face as a potent reality. It was not until I had a child to take care of that I became more aware of my own conditioning that I experienced as a child. A lot was coming to the surface which was lovely because it allowed me to see the behaviors and ways of disciplining and parenting overall that I wanted to continue to pass down, as well as those that I wanted to make peace with and completely put an end to repeating. Self-realization plus breast feeding. Get the fuck out of here. Alas, I loved being mommy and I could not stop seeking even if I wanted to at that point, so I kept on with both. Any practice of the information I was consuming was done with others, and my daughter was not someone, in my view, with whom I could practice what I was learning. Of course, that was not at all the case; but in the beginning of my seeking, that belief was the foundation of why there continued to be resistance regarding my daughter, in spite of all that I was remembering about myself. Because my core belief regarding parenting at that stage in my awakening was that it would hinder my realization, I repeated many lessons until I saw that belief for the nonsense that it was.

The teachers that I was gaining much insight from did not have children nor did a lot of the beings that I was interacting with who were seeking as well, which made it easier for me to separate parenthood from self-realization. It also seemed to be the one thing that consistently knocked me out of alignment. Later I realized of course that my child and parental responsibilities were guiding me to all the places where my awareness was needed most. I was given the perfect relationship to both see and practice overcoming my conditioning. Your child will show you all of your blind spots. That is how divine the bond between you and your child is. No need to ask anyone for a reflection. As a parent, you get one daily.

My relationship with my daughter was bringing to the surface all my shit. All of it. Everything that needed to be cleared out our relationship was bringing it up. When I did not want to see what was being brought to the surface, I would project all that I thought I knew onto my significant other at the time. That is right. When my daughter was about nine months old, I got into a relationship with someone and would turn to that relationship instead of within. How did that go? Perfectly, in that the relationship did the same thing that my daughter was doing - which was bringing up all my shit to be seen and accepted, so that the real inner work could be done.

After a few years of projecting my own pain onto my partner and choosing to not see my own toxicity for what it was, I ended that relationship. I thought that ending that relationship would be what allowed me to stay in alignment and be the parent I knew myself to be consistently because, of course, the only reason I was not was because of the relationship and my partner's toxicity, right? Wrong. It was as if that relationship was the last straw. I only had one option and that was to take full responsibility of my entire life. Each choice, each word, and each action.

Our relationship with our children will show us who we really are regardless of who we say we want to be, or who we act like in front of others. It is a potent relationship and there is no place to hide. For me, at first, I just saw it as a typical parent-child relationship where there were great and loving times and then there were times when the child did not listen; and no matter how centered the parent, the child inevitably knocks the parent off kilter. I was so entrenched in my seeking that I could not see that if I focused more on application of the information I was consuming, more so than consumption of the information itself, my daughter would then be easily identifiable as my greatest asset to self-mastery. It was when I surrendered to what my child was showing me that my entire life transformed, and I welcomed my child as a guide in assisting in my remembrance of my divinity. There even came a time where I was excited for the moments of resistance because I knew that was my green light to act how I wanted to be as a mother, and not how I was conditioned.

She is still guiding me deeper with every interaction that we have. There is no end to this journey. There is only breakthrough after breakthrough to more of who we are. I realized that I did not just have a child but that I gave birth to my greatest teacher in physical form. The challenges that I had with my child were the pathway to acceleration in all areas of my life. In tuning in to the triggers brought about within our relationship and making that a focal point of where the inner work was required, I not only transformed my relationship with my child but was also able to clear resistance within and transform my relationship with all aspects of my life.

I AM responsive, not reactive

Everyone here on Earth is powerful beyond measure and capable of living a life of their dreams, whether they are seeking realization or not. Whether they are religious, spiritual, or have no belief in a higher power at all. Labels are nothing more than labels. What you are at your core came before the label. No label can fully express what you truly are. If you have a child, then you gave yourself the key in physical form to both anchor and radiate to this planet who you truly are while incarnate. You are unconditional love incarnate and when we let love lead us in how we parent we cannot go wrong.

Resistance is felt when we are not being true to who we are in any given moment. When we are not aware that what we are feeling is because we are acting in a way that is not in alignment with who we truly are, then we suffer. We also tend to blame someone or something for that feeling. Whatever or whomever we want to blame is really a catalyst for our growth and is showing us where we need to let go. There are cords, so to speak, binding us to that thing and causing us to act from fear and separation. We are being called in those moments to cut those cords. We are being called in those moments to let go.

When I let go of how I thought things as a single mom were supposed to be, I was able to accept how things were and then create things to be how I wanted. The programming that is rampant in the collective regarding being a single parent is chock full of expectations, and being a victim if those expectations are not met. What I learned through my own experience was that the only thing that was ever in the way of a fulfilled and joyous life was me. I realized that no one owed me anything. It has only ever been my choices that ever led me to wherever I am in the present moment. I owed it to myself to accept what is; and know that what is, is what was best for me and my child. Only then was I able to see the evidence of the situation I was in as divine.

Are you not receiving child support? Then you are not meant to, or you would be.

Is the non-custodial parent not calling or visiting your child often? They are not supposed to be, or they would be.

Are you getting nowhere with your attempts to be in a relationship again with the non-custodial parent of your child? You are not supposed to be with them right now, or you would be.

At some point, we must ask ourselves, "What does my wanting these things cause me to do? Do I want to continue to behave this way? How would I behave if I no longer thought I needed these things?" It is not about being passive, but being free. Free to live our lives without suffering because of what someone else is or is not doing.

The relationship my daughter has with her father would never have happened if I continued to act from a place of pain and need. When we think someone owes us something, we are going to suffer. No matter how much the mind attempts to justify someone owing us, we will suffer if our happiness is dependent on something or someone outside of us. Our children are no exception.

We have been conditioned to believe that our children must be and act in ways that please us, and we suffer when they do not. When your child refuses to change their clothes because what they are wearing is their favorite outfit and you have your reasons why they should change some aspect of their chosen outfit and you start to express anger, you are being called to let go. Your child is acting as a catalyst to which your chosen response will either strengthen your bondage or grant you liberation. Your chosen response will strengthen and affirm your need to control, or strengthen your ability to allow, trust, and surrender to knowing everything is okay.

Letting go is like a muscle. The more you practice doing so in moments where you usually seem unable to, the easier it becomes to do so. Also, as with exercising any muscle, you see the results after continuous exercise. If you like the results you get, then you continue to do the exercise. When you do not exercise a muscle, it will weaken; and you will feel the effects of that as well. Exercising your ability to relinquish control is no different. The ability is in all of us. This exercise is required in order to be in a more relaxed state consistently, because of the conditioning we picked up along our journey since birth.

The conditioning in this example is to do what you have always done and get your way and have them change their clothes. The unknown path, which is also the path to freedom, is to do what you have never done up until now and just look at your child and be thankful they are healthy, happy, and well; and let them choose the outfit of their preference. The latter leaves you with more energy and feeling less depleted. It does wonders for your bond with your child, and it allows you to feel some freedom as well.

Whatever you give others you give yourself. We are constantly telling the universe how we want to be treated by how we treat others. Our every action and every word is us screaming, "Please treat me like this as well!" A lot of us grew up being told to give because when you give you get back tenfold. For many years, a lot of us thought that giving had to do solely with money or anything tangible. Giving is not just about money or something that can be exchanged externally. What you give energetically comes back to you tenfold. You want love, give it. To all you interact with. You want joy, spread it. You want freedom, let others be who they are without your needing to change them. You want anything, give it. We do not have to have a dime to our name to be rich. We just need to be the person in our interactions with our children and others that we want others to be with us. Your child is always interacting with the rich or poor version of you regardless of your bank account and assets. Whichever version you embody more in your moments throughout your days is the version of you that your life will reflect. Everyone is rich at their core and can live a life that reflects that wealth by identifying the behaviors and reactions that no longer serve us or are proving to not be prosperous and life giving, and then choosing behaviors and responses to life that brings us back to the wealth within that is our birthright. Doing so allows our wealth within to be reflected externally in our environment as well. There is no changing within and not seeing it reflected without.

It was so hard for me at first - when I got serious about being unconditionally loving in my expressions with my daughter, mother, and everyone else in my life. I could not believe how ridiculously hard it seemed. It seemed hard because I was afraid of feeling the pain that was being released in moments of resistance. I had to get used to letting it come up. I had to get used to feeling it all. It was the only way that I could truly no longer be controlled by my pain. I had to use it to my benefit. Doing so called for me to feel it instead of projecting the pain onto others and suppressing it. Over time, I realized that what I was calling pain was just energy that I had given negative labels. Energy that I could use to create with. Realizing this is when things got fun.

When it comes to things that cannot harm our children, it is always fun to truly consider what our children really want in the moment. When it comes to meal options, what outfits to wear, and the many other ways throughout the day that a child has an opportunity to express themselves and to wow you with that expression, it is very enjoyable to let them do what they want in those instances. It is also extremely rewarding and liberating. As we give our children more space to express themselves, we grant ourselves the same permission. When we relinquish control, we gain freedom from our actions whose sole purpose is to control another, even in the name of having good intentions. We did not have children because we had a deep calling to be a dictator. It was all love. It is all about the love, and when we make anything else a priority in the moment with our children, other than love and freedom, we suffer.

When we know that the resistance we feel in the

moment is a sign for course correction to embody more of the love that we are in that moment, then we do not suffer anymore; but instead smile and bring forth more of what we are to the world. The more we listen, and course correct in those moments, the momentum is built up towards living the life of our dreams instead of a life created based on conditioning.

We are creating, always, based on the frequency we are putting out in each moment. Your child is guiding you to and through all the energy blockages that have been preventing a constant flow. On a multidimensional and energetic level when your child triggers you, they have just gifted you with rocket fuel for your preferred reality. Will you take the surge of energy within when triggered and react as you always have thus creating the same situations, or will you take that energy and create your preference? The situations that appear in the physical with our children that seem to be the source of resistance are not what they appear. Everything is energy. Including your child. Including the mess that they made while they were eating. It is all energy appearing to your eye as a mess your child made with food. What is really happening is there is an energetic blockage of sorts that will continue to manifest in physical form in as many ways as necessary for you to clear it. In this example, it is manifesting as your child creating a mess while eating. So, what to do? Well, what you choose to do is going to be based on who you are choosing to be. Resist and become more of your conditioned self or choose in that moment to embody the parent you prefer to be and manifest more evidence of that becoming by doing so. You want to be an unconditionally loving parent?

Here is your opportunity today, one of many I am sure, to express that as who you are choosing to be. What would an unconditionally loving being do in this moment? They would not react based on conditioning but would instead respond in any of the infinite ways that are available in that moment. Making that decision takes you and your child further along the life path of your creation based on who you are choosing to be. You are quite literally changing the course of you and your child's future each time you make a decision from a place of who you prefer to be as a parent instead of who you have been conditioned to be over time. You also, in that moment, are clearing the blockage that manifested that situation that brought resistance to your awareness to begin with. When you clear it out, you make space for more manifestations based on your preference to occur. Soon enough, you look forward to those moments between you and your child and you see them as huge opportunities to accelerate in all areas of your life.

There are many ways to creatively use the highly potent surge of energy felt when triggered by our children. Our children are guiding us to everything we ever wanted and more. In using our relationship with our children to heal and bring to light our conditioning, we are also shown that what we thought we wanted may not actually be what we want; and, instead, the healing and clearing of resistance allows space for what we are truly here to be and bring forth to emerge, which usually tends to be far greater than what we once thought we wanted.

I AM *honoring the bond with my child*

Our children come into the world sweet, cute, and cuddly; but, I assure you, they are the least of all beings that are fucking around when it comes to our growth and acceleration. They come in playful and innocent and with an extremely high frequency. That high frequency triggers your conditioning. The same thing happens when you are around any being that has integrated what they truly are into their physical form and lives a life from their being and not based on their environment. But for a lot of us, avoiding others who trigger us is a preferred option; and so is suppressing all that comes up on its own when we are in solitude. For a lot of us, we may have even kept ourselves from being in the company of others just to prevent having all that we have suppressed within come to the surface to be seen and dealt with. All that hiding is out of the window when you become a parent. There is nowhere to hide.

The high frequency, unconditional love, and complete acceptance of a child not only triggers who you think yourself to be based on programming, but a child's frequency also holds space for you to be a witness to what arises and to resolve it through consciously responding instead of reacting and keeping the loop of suffering going. Your child also, unlike conditioned beings, allows you chance after chance to resolve anything and everything that arises.

Parenting is co-creation at its finest. Whether or not the relationship is being used in that way consciously, it is still manifest for the purpose of healing and amplification of who you truly are on this physical plane. Who you truly are has no need for security, validation, or control. Those are the very things that will be shed for you to experience the preferred relationship with your child. We want to love our children unconditionally and we want that for ourselves as well; but, in order to love in that way, we are going to have to let go of all behaviors that stem from the need for security, validation, and control. If we do not shed in that way, then we will continue to experience resistance with our children. What I have found is that we not only must let go in this way with our children, but that we must let go of our need to control and seek validation in every aspect and with all beings. Once you start to see the magic that occurs when you are in a state of flow with your child, you will not settle for anything less in the relationships with any other being in your life. Your child is your guide to the remembrance of your sovereignty; and, once your own sovereignty is remembered and acknowledged, you can then acknowledge the sovereignty of all others.

The way that we have perceived the parent-child dynamic over the years is extremely mundane, compared to what I experience on a day to day basis with my child. There are no words to properly convey the magic that is available when we no longer see our children as an obligation, burden, or responsibility, but instead as a creation that is free to be exactly as he or she is. Nothing is ever as it seems. Having a child included. For many, there are logical reasons as to why a child was born. One parent may say their child was planned because it was time to start a family. Another parent may believe that it is the natural order of things to have children, so, although not planned, it was time.

There are many other reasons people believe a child has entered their world either by birth, adoption, or the other myriad ways a child is created. I tell you that your child is here because you wanted more in this life in all aspects and your child was manifest to assist in clearing out all that was preventing everything you ever wanted from emerging into the physical. I tell you that your child is the biggest ally of your life and the key to unlocking the power within so that you can do what it is that you came here to do. I tell you that the relationship with your child is divine and when it is seen and honored as such in each moment, you will see magic unfold in your life beyond your wildest imagination. Your child is your guide.

I AM *powerfully on my path*

In 2012, a series of events caused me to distance myself from everyone and everything that had been normal to me for so long. I was being pulled into isolation and whenever I went against that pull something would occur that showed me that spending time alone was what was necessary at that point in time.

For years I had rarely spent time alone. I was always in the company of others and although I enjoyed being social, I felt alone most of that time. For all my life three things were easy for me to express: unconditional love, forgiveness, and curiosity. I was able to easily forgive no matter what happened. I had an ability to be present with someone who did something to hurt me and genuinely act like it never happened with no need for an apology. I was also a very curious child and that curiosity never went away as I got older. It was always evident as a child that life was a lot more peaceful and fun when people were unified and not focused on how they were different, better than, or less than others. I was very intrigued from an early age with how it seemed that so many preferred drama over peace and laughter. Not only my peers, but adults as well.

I did not know what I wanted to do with my life after high school, but I knew what I did not want to do; and was never good at doing things I did not want to do. Anytime I tried to force myself into a box that was the right thing to do by society's standards, it would not last. I left three different colleges, and the last college I left three separate times. I went back each time solely because it seemed it was the only way to get anywhere beyond where I was at that time, and because it was what pleased my parents. Both reasons deep down seemed like bullshit. It felt like bullshit that going to college and sitting in front of professors for four to six more years was the only way to live an amazing life and it also felt like bullshit to be in a classroom for all of those years again to make someone else happy. It was always short-lived because, as I stated before, I have never been able to do anything for a long period of time, if at all, that I did not want to do. However, I have always been able to give more than my all towards things that I did want to do. As a child, this attribute was not perceived as being responsible or beneficial; but, it is what saved me from a life of conformity, creating a life from limited beliefs, and not realizing my limitless nature.

From the outside looking in, it may have seemed as though I could not commit to anything or that I lacked discipline and the ability to follow through; however, what was truly happening was I was not able to stay on a path that did not excite me. I was not able to stick to a path just because it pleased my parents or was typical next steps for someone my age at the time. I felt that if I did follow the path of conformity society seemed to prefer, that I would need a lot of weed to assist. I knew deep down that there was a life for me that did not involve the dependency on marijuana to really enjoy it.

In 2013, I met a woman who was retiring. She was soon to start waitressing at a restaurant part-time while selling her crystals, jewelry, and other items online. She was working at the company I was working for at the time and was in town to teach me the role she was retiring from. After training and a few conversations throughout the weeks we spent in the office together, she requested my address because she wanted to send me a gift before she headed back home to Portland, Oregon. I gave her my address and forgot all about doing so as time passed. I did not see that woman again after our initial meeting, due to her retiring…and my being laid off shortly after I arrived, because the company decided to keep the position I was hired and trained for in Portland, Oregon, instead of migrating it to Atlanta, Georgia, where I was living at the time. There was a two-week period in between being laid off and being hired at a different company. During that time off, I received a package at my apartment. It was from the woman I met briefly at the company from which I had just been laid off. I opened the package and saw a DVD titled The Secret. I had never heard of it and popped it into the DVD player, and I remember that I was not too impressed with the production quality; and, after thinking I got the gist of the movie after about fifteen minutes, I turned it off.

Within the following week I saw copies of the book version of the movie, which I did not know existed, at a Barnes and Noble book store; and, while visiting a friend, she asked if I had seen the movie. When I told her that I saw some of it but did not finish it, she insisted that we watch it that evening. About a week after watching that movie, I was starting to watch more of Abraham Hicks on YouTube. The information that came through Esther Hicks resonated and all I knew at that time was that I was excited about it and that I was going to consume a lot of that information, and more like it, to manifest everything I want.

Manifestation. That is what it was all about for me at that time. This perhaps is also why I had no desire to read anything that had to do with inner work. I had no desire to learn about chakras. I had no desire to do anything except consume this information and any other materials that resonated and were similar in nature. This changed over time and I soon found more gratification in seeking the depth behind what Esther Hicks was speaking about. I then began my quest for self-realization. My life did not drastically change until years later when embodiment was more important than consuming and seeking. After Abraham Hicks, I was led to many other teachers who were lovely permission slips for me to transcend seeking and step into mastery.

In late 2014, I found out that I was pregnant and, although I was excited as my pregnancy progressed, I believed that a child would hinder the perceived progress I had made spiritually. Really, I was afraid I would not be able to consume as much as I had been. Back then, consumption equaled realization. I still was not doing the one thing necessary for transformation, and that was to apply the information that was being consumed in my everyday life. What I found out later, when application was becoming more important than consumption, was that even with application, if there was still judgement and fear within, my life could only transform so far.

In 2015, my daughter was born, and, in hindsight, it is evident that everything surrounding her birth, including the conditions before her conception, were catalysts for my awakening. I had set some powerful intentions when I was in my "manifesting" phase and even before. I was getting everything I ever wanted and more, but in the form of catalysts that would wake me up to my true nature and clear out all that was preventing my life from becoming transformed and created from my being, instead of my conditioning.

Catalysts were necessary because, as I stated earlier, I was not at all excited about educating myself on chakras, healing, or inner work. I held strong to the notion that consuming information regarding self-realization and following teacher after teacher who resonated was enough. I was not reading much at all about healing, inner work, or chakras. It did not seem necessary and deep down I did not want it to be necessary. I was happy with the bubbly feelings I felt consuming the information that seemed to be enough to elevate me higher than where I was before I came across such information. It certainly felt better than anything I felt before 2012, which is also why I had no problem with the hamster wheel that was consumption. I was seeking more and more material that resonated and finding just that; however, without application, there is just a high that we get on the resonance of what we are reading, written by those who actually embodied what it is that they are pointing to in their teachings.

I AM responsible for my own transformation

When we have a child, sometimes we tend to think that being a parent is going to transform us. We think that being a parent now means that everything before that new role is washed away and we are starting life anew. Sometimes that belief can even be what prompts some to have children on purpose. A child will change everything. Yes, in my experience, there is some truth to a child changing everything. However, not in the way that spontaneously heals everything within that had been suppressed. More so along the lines of a child bringing to the surface everything prior to their birth that had not been looked at, accepted, and cleared. The anger, frustration, and other emotions that we feel when triggered really need space. Those thoughts that we do not like but seem to keep haunting us. Those emotions we judge others for expressing and do anything to suppress when they arise within us. They just need some space. When we do not allow them to rise and give them space while witnessing them come and go, they go away for a bit but will always return. Feeling irritated, angry, sad, etc., is not wrong even when you feel those emotions regarding your child. What is not natural is denying those emotions. We can, over time, master the art of allowing anger to rise and witnessing as it comes and goes without reacting from that anger; but instead, responding to our children after it has passed when there is clarity.

It is such a blessing that the relationships we have with our children are so sacred and divine because we are being called to lovingly utilize them in each interaction to not only maintain alignment, but to also constructively use the energy that arises within when triggered by them. To be proactive and not reactive with the energy that is both able to create and destroy. The surge of energy that comes up from within when triggered will either be blocked or allowed to flow and if you allow it to flow you can direct that flow with your attention. It is time to not only realize who we are but to actualize. To not only grasp that we are creators conceptually but to be the creators we are. Our children are guiding us to this ability and to the steady maintenance of this ability.

I smoked a lot of marijuana before my daughter was conceived, but I always knew that my habit would change when I had a child. Not for any other reason other than at the time I knew that I would function better with a newborn if I was not high. Ultimately, it was clarity that I wanted for her and myself. I wanted to be as clear as possible while taking care of her. Allowing our emotions that we have reacted to for so long, to our own detriment, to come and go and then responding to our children from a place of clarity not only allows us the bond we truly want with our children, but also shows them that it is possible to be mature in that way. When children see that level of awareness in their parents they catch on early and start to mimic that behavior by choosing themselves to respond instead of reacting. There is no hiding from ourselves. Having a child gives you the opportunity to see yourself much more clearly. Your child will show you all your blind spots. That is how divine the bond between you and your child is. No need to ask anyone for a reflection. As a parent, you get one daily. Knowing the type of bond you want for you and your child is powerful in that it is a vision that you can hold daily while interacting with your child, and use it as a gauge regarding responses. Some behaviors match that vision. Some do not. Behaving in ways that match your vision more often will increasingly bring that vision to life.

I started my story in 2012. However, between the years of 1989 and 2012, there was some laughter, some happy times, and a lot of suffering. At age 16, I started to use marijuana, alcohol, and sex to suppress a lot of things that happened in my life up to that point, which had never been given any real space to be acknowledged, accepted, and cleared. At the time, I did not look at my behavior as suppression, but it was. I distanced myself from my family and maintained many toxic friendships and relationships, even though they may not have appeared as such on the surface. My actions showed that I felt that everything I did not want to think, or feel, was all best swept under the table with substances, avoidance, and denial. Try as you may, nothing is truly ever really suppressed. It all comes up at some point. There really is no hiding from yourself. When you have a child, this does not change. Everything that you were not willing to look at prior to becoming a parent will still need to be faced and accepted to be transcended. In order to be the parent you want to be and are becoming, you are going to have to lovingly get over the aspect of you that believes any limiting belief that prevents your ability to see how ridiculously worthy you are of the life that the highest version of you as a parent lives.

In 2012, I felt a strong pull to start to isolate and was not sure of the reason. It is no coincidence that some of the most catalyzing circumstances and relationships occurred in my life before, during, and after my daughter's birth. It was all love. Unconditional love and my daughter. Even though I was not at all thinking about her conception that would occur a few years later, there was a lot of preparation and introspection occurring in my life that would allow me to be the version of myself I wanted to be for my child. After my child's birth, I was still calling forth more catalysts due to me not paying attention to what the resistance in my life was telling me, or acknowledging that I was the only one getting in my own way. This is a game of love, and love has no limits. Whatever it takes for you to see that the only way out is to go within will be called forth until you pay attention and see what the resistance in your life is showing you. I would not have wanted it any other way. Life is truly magical when you pay attention and use catalysts to your advantage by being the creator that you are in that moment; and responding to your children, others, and all circumstances in your life in the way you would prefer, instead of how you have been conditioned.

As if that was not enough that some of the most catalyzing circumstances and relationships occurred in my life before, during, and after my daughter's birth, the relationship with my child itself was no exception. My daughter was basically saying, "Hey mom, so I see you are not trying to do the inner work necessary to release the resistance and conditioning that your life is looping from, so here I am. I am here to bring up everything that keeps you a slave to your mind and its conditioning and, as I'm your daughter, you have no choice but to see it as it comes up; and if you should choose to ignore it and continue to suppress it, that is okay. I will love you unconditionally and let you do so as many times as you can stand it." And that is exactly what she did. She led me through an inner cleansing and allowed me to fall in love with the inner work to the point of no longer seeing it as work. I knew the relationship I was meant to experience with my child, and it was one of unconditional love. I would not experience

the relationship I knew was meant for my child and
I if I did not first go within and start to do the work.

I AM *worthy regardless of my past actions*

What should have been normal all along is now made to seem as though it is special. Being aware of how you respond to life has been labeled as conscious, spiritual, or many of the other fluffy terms used. Instead, to be aware of how you respond to life and to see that your actions create your reality is more so a conversation that has not yet been normalized but is common sense. What you do in each moment determines the next moment. A book in the self-development section of Barnes and Noble should not be needed to understand that. However, it is not something that is really spoken on to the degree necessary for one to see early on that they are the creator and not the victim; always, and with no exceptions. My family sure was not throwing those statements around as I was a child. I never once heard, "You are the creator of your life." Ever. For it to be the truth and to not hear it ever until adulthood shows that although I can see it as common sense now, it is still uncommon among the collective. The energy from which you do anything in each moment determines the energy you carry into the next moment. Now is the most important moment and the moment from which all is created. Anything you want in the future is attained by first becoming the version of yourself that has it in the future, while in this now moment. You do not get the relationship you want with your child and then become the parent who has that relationship. You become the parent in this now moment that has the relationship of your preference with your child and then the relationship with your child mirrors back who you have become. This is beautiful because that means as a parent, there is never a need nor true benefit in criticizing the parent you have been in the past. We can now delete all shame and guilt about our past actions and invite ourselves to feel into the infinite potentials available to us now, in this moment, regarding how to respond to our children and life in general, instead of reacting from our conditioning. The only thing that ever matters is the parent you are choosing to be right now. The moment that realization of the now moment being all that matters really sinks in, there is so much forgiveness that takes place in an instant because you know that anything you did prior to what you do in this now moment is null and void. No matter what it is. There are no exceptions to this. This may not sit well with anyone who wants you to stay stuck in the past because they themselves are stuck in the past, but that is for them to reflect on. As far as you are concerned, the moment you realize that now is all that matters and that the past is gone and the future is being created based on who you are choosing to be and respond as in this moment, there is no more reason to regret past actions or to feel like a victim of past decisions. Your focus is shifted to what you are being in the moment. Did you yell at your child .2

seconds ago? Even that does not matter. That moment is in the past and holds no relevance to right now. None. When you judge yourself for anything that happened even .2 seconds ago, you suffer. You suffer because you are living in an illusion. The past is gone, and you are still clinging to it. That impacts the way we respond to our children. Children do not cling to the past. Children are very free flowing in that what happened a moment ago is done, as far as they are concerned, and they are just ready to see what is happening now. My child is five and it is very evident that she is rarely focused on the past unless it is a memory that she is in love with. For quite some time, she has shown that she is aware that whatever is going on right now in the moment is where all of the juice is, and she even knows that it is the precursor for future happenings; and that is where our children keep their attention. They are guiding us back to that way of being.

When you practice letting go after reacting based on conditioning, it benefits you and your child and brings you both to the present moment where all your power is. At first, yes, forgiving yourself after reacting in a moment with your child instead of consciously choosing your preferred response is beneficial and much better than beating yourself up about it. Everything in the past has made us who we are now, which are beings who want to operate differently as parents than we have been conditioned to. This desire in us that our programming has inspired is a blessing to the generations that come forth after us. So we thank the past and we thank our parents. We thank everything that we never imagined we would be both forgiving of and thankful for. To harbor judgement and vengeance towards those who played a role in our programming limits our capacity to actualize our limitlessness and makes it about us. This isn't about us. Feeling guilt, shame, and regret about our own behavior as parents does the same. However, as you continue this path of being the parent you want to be, you will find that even the forgiveness is not needed. You will slip and react towards your child and then, because of all your practice up to that point, immediately hop back into alignment as the parent you know yourself to be. You will not spend a moment dwelling on even just one minute ago because you will be so into being with your child how you want to be instead. You start to really see the effects of how who you are being right now in this moment is creating the future for you, thus impacting the future of the relationship of you and your child. Even forgiving yourself is no longer where you want to invest your precious, finite, linear time; because you do not want to waste too many moments, if any at all, not being what you want your life to reflect more of. The action you choose to take now is all that matters and makes the past obsolete and is highly indicative of your future.

PRACTICE #2

The Hug-It-Out Method

I want to share a practical and easy to practice exercise that I would go as far as to say brings about instant manifestation. In all actuality, you are always instantly manifesting. There are so many teachers, programs, and modalities that are centered around "how to manifest", but the funny thing is, you are constantly manifesting. You have never *not* been manifesting. Everything around you are manifestations and if you are breathing you will be manifesting instantly moment to moment, because you have never *not* been a creator. Instant manifestation is nothing new. It's just that the concepts regarding manifestation may be newer to us in this lifetime, because they are not concepts a lot of us were raised hearing about amongst those in our immediate surroundings. However, the truth behind the concept is nothing new at all.

You are just remembering that truth and the concepts are pointers to that truth. The exercise that I am mentioning to you here is extremely easy and practical. The instant manifestation that I speak of is the manifestation of your preference. You are always manifesting, but are you always manifesting what you want? This practice that I am about to describe overrides conditioning in a very simple way. It is so simple that it may sound a bit ridiculous to some; but we are at a point in time where I do not feel as though making the process of overcoming one's conditioning more complex is something that we can afford to do. Making something simple overly complex has become an art form of sorts. There are so many words that have been expressed verbally and written to point us back to our true nature. However, when it comes to actual transformation and a true shift in perspective, application must be placed above consumption of information.

At some point, one gets to a place where they respect and are grateful for all of the beautiful pointers they have read and heard but they want to see it in the physical embedded in their lives amongst those they interact with. That is when embodiment is placed above consumption. Action is called for to see all the work you have done on the inside manifest externally. If you want to love unconditionally while alive, then you are going to have to act in that way as well. Your deeds, words, and thoughts must align to bring all the love that you are here.

The resistance we feel with others is due to our actions and words not synchronizing with what we both want and know ourselves to be, and our not paying attention to how we feel. When we are coming from the space we want to come from with our children, we will feel it and it will feel good and our children will feel it as well. I stated before that this practice that I am mentioning is quite simple. The only thing that may be difficult is your willingness to commit. You must be committed to the practice. It is life changing, but you must commit. It is easy to revert to conditioning. Living the conditioned life is extremely easy. When you are around family or friends or even alone with your child and your child does something that brings up conditioned thought forms that lead to conditioned reactions that lead to conditioned ways of discipline, it is very easy to revert to reactivity. To live a life of our dreams, we are going to have to do things we have not yet done before. We are going to have to respond in ways that we have not responded before.

The life of your dreams does not manifest by you continuing to react to life the same way you always have. The life of your dreams does not manifest by you reacting to life at all, but by you choosing how to respond based on what feels good to you. You bring that version of you here to the now moment in the environment you are currently in, and then the environment shifts accordingly. When you are with your child, what you are going to do with this practice is whenever there is tension no matter how small, give them a hug and a kiss. That is the practice. I do not care how small the resistance is that is felt. Give them a hug and a kiss. You can choose to do just a hug if you would like, but this practice specifically suggests a hug and a kiss. Why take one aligned action when you can take two? As you continue in this practice, your awareness of resistance will heighten. You will catch it earlier and earlier and those hugs and kisses will be your response sooner and sooner. I could say if you do this for only ten hours with your child you will be blown away by what you witness as a result, and how it impacts other aspects of your life as well.

No matter how dramatic we are when we tell our stories, our children do not trigger us twenty-four seven. So for the sake of allowing more time for situations to arise that bring about resistance, I will say if you commit to this practice for twenty-four hours, you will feel an elevation in vibration and you will have experienced enough magic from this exercise to choose to commit to it long-term. If you do this exercise for seventy-two hours, you will have experienced enough of the magic of this exercise and your willingness to commit to overriding your conditioning to commit to it or any other practice that is used in place of reactivity for life. If you do this practice for seven days, you will have experienced enough magic from this exercise to commit to it with everyone in your life. Where you are on your journey prior to being excited about this exercise will determine the timeframe between applying it and choosing to apply it to everyone in your life. It may be seven days of application or it may only take one day for you to want to hug all beings at the point of tension.

I would like to point out that discernment is called for when applying the hug and kiss technique with others that you do not know intimately. It may be a physical hug and a kiss, a physical hug only, or a *vibrational* hug and kiss, where you apply it but do not do so physically. All of which bring about the same affect and elevate your response, override your conditioned reaction in the moment, and bring about a higher timeline in the physical than that of your conditioned self. With your children and partners, I suggest the actual physical hug and kiss. This exercise is life changing. There will be times when the other does not want to receive the hug and kiss and that is beautiful. In those moments, we do not judge them not wanting to receive the hug and kiss, but we do honor where we are in the moment and where we have elevated to. We have elevated to responding with love; and if that is not where the other would like to respond from, that is perfectly okay. We will not descend in frequency because of that, but instead we will see them there, be compassionate, and whatever comes next will be from a loving place, even if that means postponing the conversation until later.

This is not about telling you what to do after you have elevated the vibration of the interaction by choosing to respond with a hug and a kiss physically or vibrationally. Once you elevate the frequency in such a way, you are in the unknown. You have transcended conditioned behavior in that moment and are riding the waves of your sovereignty in the moment and are able to freely be in action that which you are choosing to become. Whatever action you take after transcending your conditioning in that moment is going to benefit all parties involved. You will be compassionate because you will be able to see after your aligned action that if the other is not welcoming of that loving embrace, either physically or vibrationally, it is not personal; but is, instead, because of their own conditioning, which you yourself have experienced and continue to transcend. There is no pity or judgement towards the other adult or child, but instead there is love and understanding that would not be available if you had chosen to react yourself from your own conditioning. Whether they are receptive to your chosen state of being or not, you still have allowed them to see an example of the embodiment of love. You have chosen to show them what is possible and available to them as well.

Your child is not conditioned the way a fifteen, twenty-five, thirty, or sixty-year-old is conditioned. People who are older have much heavier conditioning and have experienced more trauma. I highly recommend keeping a journal to start so that you can log your experiences with this practice daily. Writing what you experience with this practice is powerful, and it is also beautiful to reflect on previous journal entries as days and weeks go by and your life transforms because of the practice. Your child is going to be very expressive regarding your new way of responding. It is going to take them by surprise the more you implement this practice because your child has been on this journey with you since day one, so they have experienced your conditioned reactions. Responding differently in the moment is going to be equally as life changing for them as it is for you. Wherever you and your child choose to go after your new way of responding is how you choose to go from there; but whatever comes from it is going to be higher in vibration than had you continued to react from conditioning.

This practice, albeit profoundly simple, is not to be taken lightly. It is life changing and I speak from my own experience. I applied it to my own life as soon as it came through me. I cannot stress enough the benefits of committing to this practice. No matter how evolved or embodied you know yourself to be, there are always more subtle layers where love can be infused.

I AM *powerful*

You are immensely powerful beings and the resistance you feel with your children is an indicator of where you are leaking some of that power. You have never been triggered. You have only ever shown yourself where you continue to give your power away. Your children, although they may not have said this, want you fully charged. When you are fully in your power, they get to learn by your example how to be fully in their power. Power is another term for sovereignty - someone who is in control of themselves and loves their lives enough to create it on their own terms, based on who they choose to be. Knowing who they are and not affected by what another being says or does but marches to the beat of their own drum unapologetically.

How do we want our children to express themselves when we are no longer here? Do we want them abiding by the program? Working a 9-5 they do not like to make ends meet? Do we want them following guidance from others who do not know themselves deeply? No. So why would we settle for that way of living ourselves? Why would we provide that as an example? As we continue to do the inner work, we can stand in our power and express ourselves authentically as the sovereign beings that we are and create our lives accordingly. Our children cannot comprehend why that is not how we would be living anyways. They are not yet aware of the fact that a lot of what they witness their parents do is not by choice. So, they think that their parents are choosing to do these things and in turn want to do it too. We are choosing to do things we do not want, and it is not until we step into our power and make choices based on what we want to do and what feels best to us that we will provide a different example for our children. One of freedom and unconditional love. Unconditional love, because you must love yourself and honor what you want to do in each moment to make decisions that reflect that. There is no freedom without unconditionally loving yourself. That comes first. Our children are never triggering us. They are showing us where we are and inviting us to level up. They know that we are capable. They do not see us in the same limited way we have been conditioned to see ourselves. They see you in your magnitude. In your glory and magnificence. With each trigger they are seeing if we want to expand into more of our limitlessness or stay small.

I AM

Needing some type of external validation regarding you and your child's relationship becomes a thing of the past when you start to bring your awareness to the parent you are being in each moment. Every action you take as the parent you prefer to be regarding your child in each moment adds more momentum to the timeline of your preference. What do you envision your relationship with your child to be like in five years? What is your favorite vision of the bond between you and your child? When you act how you envision yourself to be right now, you bring that vision here to the present moment and allow your child to experience that version of you. Why wait five years from now to be the parent you want to be and to have the unconditionally loving relationship you want with your child? Be it now.

When your deeds start to align with the thoughts you have about the parent you want to be, then everything in your life will adjust to that new way of being. Reading information such as this or anything else that is empowering is lovely and beneficial to a degree, but the real power lies within your willingness to embody what is being discussed here. The magic is always in the application of that which resonates with you. When you envision yourself as a parent and when you see the relationship between you and your child in the future, what do you see?

Do you see you and your children having a remarkably close, transparent, unconditionally loving, and authentic bond in the future? Do you want that now? It is all possible and well on its way, but action on your part is going to be called for. Act as the version of yourself that you see when you visualize the relationship of your preference with your child. You may never get an Oscar for owning your lead role in your life as the creator of all conditions that surround you, but an Oscar is nothing in comparison to living a life day in and day out that feels amazing and that is reflecting back to you your preference. Your child is calling forth action.

Having a child places you on an accelerated path due to the many actions you are called to take on both your behalf and theirs. If acting and responding as the person you are choosing to be is what creates your reality, then with a child you now have double the opportunities to do that. The thoughts we have about the feelings we feel when triggered are a program. We were conditioned to label these feelings negatively. We are being called to flip the script on those labels. The option in each moment that you are triggered by your children is to either give away or amplify your power. Use your triggers to your benefit. They are there for you anyways. Redirect the energy that comes up when triggered. Create with it.

Sure, without a child I would still be able to accelerate in my expansion, but I may have needed to do more or be more places to get the interactions going that allowed me to choose who I am becoming over my conditioned way of behaving. It's not that life as a parent is harder than life before you have children. Becoming a parent is a self-initiation. Your enlightenment is inevitable with or without children. However, having a child allows for you to take a ride on the accelerated path. Everything you were ignoring and suppressing gets turned up a few notches. For your benefit. Your child is guiding you back to your heart. To the remembrance of who you really are. Constantly giving you opportunities to be who you want to be instead of who you have been conditioned to be. With a child, I have a growing human right here with me 7 days a week 24 hours a day to give me all the opportunities and more to be my preference. If you were supposed to be a monk, you would be somewhere playing that role. As a mother, you are being called to action. There is no way around it. In being the parent you prefer to be, you start to apply that way of being to all areas of your life and become the version you prefer yourself to be across the board, thus creating a life of your dreams.

Your life as you know it now must shift if you shift. When you make any change in any way, life responds to you differently. Your child will show you quickly that if you cannot achieve the award-winning performance of your choosing regarding parenting, then you will face blockages in other areas of your life as well. You are writing the script each moment with each choice you make. The more loving the choices, the more you love your life.

It is not about being conscious or spiritual. What type of parent do you want to be? Be that right this very moment. With every interaction with those in your immediate environment, be the parent you want to be. Bring that vision here to this physical reality right now, in every interaction. You do not have to wait; and if you think you have to wait on some things in your life to look a certain way in order to then be the parent you want to be, then you will be waiting until you choose not to. Your child is your guide but is still taking cues from who you are being in this moment. Being the version of yourself you prefer to be as a parent manifests a reflection of that. I am talking about instant manifestation here. There is a lag in linear time, of course, for the larger manifestations as it all has to come about in a seemingly logical way, based on what you believe to be logical; however, you very instantly are able to see the effects of responding to your children the way you prefer as opposed to how you have been conditioned to react. Your child takes no time to reflect this decision back to you. When you have yelled at your children in a particular situation repeatedly and now, instead of yelling, you are leaning in for a hug, it will be surprising to those most used to your conditioned behavior.

In those moments where no matter how much you maintain your preferred state of being they still seem to not be reflecting back to you your preference, that is okay and not your concern. Your only concern in this moment is being the parent you want to be in that moment regardless of what your children are doing. They will eventually catch on as long as you stay committed. They have not seen you maintain that state of being in that situation before. So what is called for on your part is nothing more than continuing to show them you mean business and to continue to be the parent you choose to be in that moment. Ultimately, it is your desire to be who you know yourself to be and your devotion to responding as that being that will cause a drastic transformation in your life. Without the desire and devotion, consuming information such as this will resonate; but the embodiment which is what brings about the transformation will be kept at bay.

I AM *choosing love*

Your child as your guide, as you are well aware, gives you many opportunities to choose more love, more joy, more of how you prefer to be over any conditioning each time they do something that gives rise to emotions that once may have caused you to react. Your personal trainer does not give up on you when you do not meet your physical goals. Your doctor does not tell you not to come back to his office when they see that your blood pressure or other metrics are not where they would prefer them to be. Your child as your guide to be the person you came here to be does not give up on you when you step back into old patterns and react from conditioning. They will give you as many opportunities to choose who you are at your core over who you have been programmed to be.

Who you want to be in every aspect of your life is exactly who you really are, and the resistance you feel is because you are yelling at your child and deep down you do not want to yell. You are spanking your child and deep down you do not want to. You are upset and you do not want to be. Why do we do anything we do not want to? Why do we repeatedly do things that do not feel good? Because we have been conditioned. It has become a pattern. A habit, if you will, to do things we do not want to do and then to justify it to feel better about doing what we do not want to do. We reinforce our own suffering and then when triggered we project the pain we suppress by justifying our unconscious actions onto those closest to us. Anytime you are doing something that you want to be doing you will feel great about it; and when you do something you do not want to do you will feel bad about it.

Society has conditioned us to think that when it comes to parenting, we do what we do not want to do because we love our children and it needs to be done, even if we do not want to do it. This is bullshit. This is also why so many of us do not have healthy boundaries. As our children see us doing things that we do not want to do, they learn that life is about doing what you do not want to do. It is not. Which is why it does not feel good. It is an incredibly old way of being that has been passed down generation to generation and you are here to break that cycle. If what you are doing in any aspect of your life does not feel good, honor that and look within for some other way. Quite literally ask yourself what are the alternatives that feel good. You will receive an answer; and if it feels good and excites you, trust it. There is always another way.

You do not get anything without first being the person who has it. You must know that you are both worthy and deserving of all that comes with being who you want to be. You do get married without first being the person who proposes or accepts a proposal. You do not get the car of your dreams without first being the person who goes to the dealership and fills out the paperwork for the car. You do not get a new house without first being the individual who does what is necessary to get the new house. You do not get the unconditionally loving relationship with your child that you have always wanted until you first be, in each moment, the person who is unconditionally loving. Before doing all of that, you must first know that you are able. It is not a matter of seeing it and then being it. It is being it and then seeing it. Every triggering moment with your child is an opportunity to choose who you are at your core and who you want to be over your conditioning; and each time you choose who you wish to be over your programming, you take you and your child further along the timeline that is full of everything and everyone that is an aspect of the life of your dreams.

As you continue to free yourself of your own conditioning, you align ever more so with the pure positive energy that your children came into the world as. They came here with no programming. No conditioning. As you do the inner work, put your alignment first, and act accordingly, you and your children accelerate in all aspects of your lives. The moments you think are small and do not matter are moments that matter regarding the timeline that you are on. There is no moment that you are incarnated that does not matter. Every single moment is a moment to choose who you are and thus create from that place.

I AM beyond my conditioning

The Matrix movies were among my favorites as a child. In those movies, and even in my reading years after, I heard a lot of talk about programming and how we are programmed. It resonated, but I still was not sure about what it meant to be programmed. I soon learned that I had indeed been programmed and conditioned by society and all who had been in my immediate experience as a child. I took on their beliefs and their ways of being. This is the natural way of things. A child born to a mother who teaches the child from birth that blue is pink will grow to think blue is pink. That thought will harden into a belief. As the child turns four and goes to preschool, she will be told by her teacher that what she believes is not correct. The child will listen, but, after four years of being told one thing, it will take a while for the child to accept this new belief. The child will first have to accept the new thought and then think it often until it turns into a belief.

However, the child may face opposition because her mom is who started her on the path of blue being pink to begin with; and this child is still living at home with her mom who has no plans of changing that way of thinking. The child is in a bit of a pickle, to say the least, and will have to make her own decision. In making her own decision on the matter, she will then stand firm in it. So what seemed unfortunate with the mother instilling blue to be pink is actually very beneficial in the child's development overall, as it plays a role in the child having to eventually go within and make her own decision, which is very freeing and empowering. Although, her decision on this blue-is-pink situation may, in the end, not go over so well with her mother or her teacher, depending on what she determines to be true based on her own resonance, it will, however, go well with the child in that she will have stepped a bit more into her own sovereignty.

Realizing that the way we have been programmed is not the way we resonate with living can sometimes cause us to blame our parents and society as a whole, but actually it was all a blessing in showing us even more clearly our preference. Therefore, everything in the past has made us who we are now - which are beings who want to operate differently than we have been conditioned to operate as parents. This desire in us that our programming has inspired is a blessing to the generations that come forth after us.

Desiring to be one way but in certain triggering moments acting in another way, that I would often either regret or felt the need to apologize for, was my conditioning coming up against the version of me that I preferred to express in the moment wanting to come through. Having a child shows you the programs being held regarding parenting. You tend to have a vision before your child is born regarding the type of parent you will be and the relationship that you will have with your child when they are born. The only thing that prevents that from coming to fruition is conditioning. How you were parented as a child is embedded deeply within your subconscious mind and it takes your awareness to override the strongly held beliefs that emerge in the form of resistance. It is good to feel into how committed you feel that you truly are at being the parent you want to be instead of the parent you were conditioned to be. Asking yourself this question and authentically feeling into it and accepting what you realize from that inquiry will strengthen your devotion because the inquiry will often times show you your blind spots that you may never have seen if you did not inquire within. If you feel after inquiring that you are indeed very committed, you will still be shown the beautiful ways the devotion can be deepened. You are infinite beings. The capacity to expand is never-ending. When you choose who you really are and who you prefer to be over who you have been conditioned to be, you break cycles that have been passed down for generations; and also greatly impact the generations that come after your child.

Your choices right now have consequences that go much farther beyond you and your child. It becomes the framework of the relationship that your child will have with their child. It becomes the framework of who your child will be with their peers, thus impacting everyone they interact with. Choosing who you are in each moment is a huge responsibility with the greatest rewards and it is indeed a responsibility when you become aware that you create your reality. There is no one else to blame once this is realized. There is no more victimization. There is only you, living the conditioned life and continuing to dislike the ramifications of doing so; or you, living the unconditionally loving and creative life and enjoying all that comes with that. Those are our options. The only thing left, once you no longer perceive yourself to be a victim of the past and stand firm in your knowing that you are the creator of your reality, is knowing your power and that knowingness deepening. Our knowing can only deepen and, regardless of the responsibility, you would not choose to live life any other way. Your realization deepens forevermore because you are infinite. There is no end to remembering who you are; therefore, there is no limit to seeing more of that remembrance reflected to you.

I AM *not a victim*

The life of your dreams is not on the timeline that you create when you react. The life of your dreams is on the timeline created when you choose to respond to your child based on the parent you want to be. However, if you want to be, have, or do anything then you continue to keep yourself playing the game of wanting. One day you are going to get tired of the wanting energy and partake in the energy of being it now. You do not have to want anything, especially to be the parent you always hoped you would be. You can be that right now. You are that right now. The only thing not allowing you to experience that is believing you are not already the parent you want to be. Once you align with that belief and your actions reflect that alignment you will no longer believe otherwise and resistant thoughts that were in alignment with doubting who you are will no longer prevent you from expressing your unconditionally loving self with your children. Your child's birth was an invitation to do just that.

Everything in our lives is an invitation to be who we want to be as we interact with it. You never need your child to be anything other than who they are for you to be who you want to be in relation to them. When we are used to handing our power over to others, it can seem that our children have to be a certain way for us to be the unconditionally loving parents that we aspire to be; but that is just a belief due to conditioning.

Nothing outside of you must do a damn thing for you to be, in this moment, who you want to be. Is your child running around the house something that usually upsets you? Perfect. Conditioning says your child needs to stop for you to be "okay." For things to be how they should be, he must chill out. This line of thinking places you in a state of victimization and totally dependent on your child's behavior to determine how you should be in the moment. Your child is guiding you back home to your *self* with every triggering moment. Your child is elated you have come home to your *self* in each non-resistant moment. To my readers whose children are still toddlers, they just came out of the womb a few years ago. Think about it, they just got here, and our stability is dependent on them? When babies witness our instability, I wonder what they would say if they could speak? "Send me the fuck back!" comes to mind. Your infants and toddlers are stable when they come out of the womb. They need to be fed and cleaned, as we all do. Other than that, they are emotionally stable.

Co-dependency is a behavior that is learned. When you react negatively to your child you show yourself and your child that you are dependent on them for your sanity. When you take those moments that usually trigger you and you choose to be in that moment who you want to be, no matter what your child is doing, you cause your child to have no other choice but to respond to that version of you. You both then are co-creating a new scenario that would never have been experienced if you continued to react as you always have. We want so much for our children, but at the core of our desires for them is freedom and joy. Everyone has their own idea of what freedom looks like. To some, freedom looks like a big house and nice cars. To some, it looks like the perfect partner. To others, it looks like a lot of money in the bank. I have seen that all of those things, and more, comes when you express yourself as free first before you get the house, the partner, and the large sums of money. The version of you that is dependent on things, outside of yourself, to be a certain way in order for you to be okay in any capacity is not the version of you who has the things that you want.

Everything you want that is well on its way to you right now is going to call forth more of the version of yourself that you prefer to be. The more you respond as the parent you wish yourself to be, the more you are in a state of becoming that parent. You are also showing your child true stability which allows true stability to be an option for them as well. When you show them stability as you step into your creator shoes and create your life based on who you desire to be, and not who you have been conditioned to be, then you allow space to be held between you and your child. A beautiful space...wherein you are both sovereign and the actions of one do not lessen the love given by the other. You get to maintain who you have chosen to be in that moment and your child gets to continue to be loved by you, regardless of their behavior; and feels your acceptance of them, and gets to choose to continue in his behavior or not. Either way, they are not carrying the burden of regulating your emotions; and your sanity is not dependent on their actions. There is a beautiful space for you both to just be yourselves and accept one another.

I AM *embodying the golden rule*

Practically speaking when it comes to our children, we are making a tad bit more complex the notion of treating them in each moment the way that we want to be treated. Any way you flip it, this way of parenting is not at all what the majority were raised witnessing and experiencing. When your child asks to do something that is harmless, such as sleep with a toy under their pillow, and you say no, where is that no coming from? Habit? Conditioning? Sometimes in the moment we are not taking the time to dig that "deep," so here is another question that takes no time at all to reach the answer. If you wanted to sleep with a little toy dinosaur under your pillow right now, would you want to be free to do so? Yes, you would. So, feel that freedom wash over you as you give that same freedom to your child.

This is just one example of many throughout the day where we are offered the opportunity to give our child the freedom, acceptance, and unconditional love that we would also like and are worthy of. Every time we attempt to reframe the situation at hand with our children in this way, we free ourselves from the bondage of conditioned behavior and become more of who we prefer to be in that moment. That is what this is all about. Freedom. Embodiment. Becoming. Not *wanting* to become a better anything, but instead being it now and creating life from you being who you prefer to be; and treating our children how we want to be treated while, of course, holding their hands and taking care of their needs while they are children. Treating your child with respect and as you wish to be treated is not irresponsible. There is a saying that has been long overdue for annihilation in the parenting community, "I am your parent, not your friend." Friend means a person who one knows and with whom one has a bond of mutual affection. You are most definitely your child's friend and the only thing preventing your acknowledgment of that fact is your own conditioning and limited beliefs that were passed down to you from society, family, etc. The definition of friend typically excludes family and sexual relations which is why familial and intimate relationships have the unbelievable amount of dysfunction that they do. We are here on this planet in these bodies for a truly short period of time. It is worth inquiring within whether in that short period of time you want to be your child's friend or not.

Ask yourself what the benefits may be to you and your children's relationship if you started to view them as a friend and treat them how you would treat a friend. There may be times where others may view being a friend to your child as irresponsible, but that is because they are still very heavily programmed with the notion that, as a parent, one of your main jobs is to control your children. You will be hard pressed to find a controlling parent who themselves were not controlled as a child. Being controlling is learned behavior. It is not who we really are. We did not come out of the womb needing to be in control.

All control will be lost in the last moments before we transition. Our children are guiding us to letting go now. To being free of the need to control now. Your child is guiding you to the freedom that you are. Due to conditioning, it can be a bit hard to respond in a way that you did not experience as a child. Another reason it may be difficult is if deep down you do not feel free in any area of your life; so, it will be hard to gift another with freedom in a moment where control can be used. This is not because you do not want to gift your child with that lovely feeling of freedom, but because freedom is something that you yourself are not feeling; and may very well have not felt in an exceptionally long time.

It is hard to genuinely give what we ourselves are not experiencing. Our children are guiding us to freedom. When we allow them the freedom to be themselves and to feel free in the moment, we unlock the chains that bind us to past conditioning and gift ourselves with freedom as well, which spreads to all other areas of our lives.

I AM *applying the teachings and practices that resonate*

Life is always in flux – ever changing. There is no stagnation in life. There is only choosing in this moment who you are becoming. You are always in a state of becoming. You will never arrive at a destination of having become something. Even when you think you have become something, so long as you are breathing, even that which you think you have become is still in a state of becoming. There is no destination. You are always evolving.

When I was starting to wake up in 2012, there was a part of me, for even a few years after, that thought there was a destination. I operated as if that was the case. I was consuming so much information and expecting to see some result based on resonance with the information and the consumption of it alone. My drive in the beginning was based on my thirst for end results. My focus was more on outcomes than being present in the becoming. There was the thought that there was an end to this rabbit hole I had jumped down, and that was a cause of suffering until this lesson was learned – *there is no limit to your ability to expand and experience yourself deeper as love.* There is no limit to the depth of your realization. This is beautiful; and once application and embodiment of what resonates with you conceptually is kicked into high gear, we see that there is also equally no limit to our ability to actualize.

You are limitless and there is no limit to your ability to see that limitlessness reflected to you in the physical as well. The vastness realized within must manifest without.

In each moment, there is only a choice to react based on conditioning or to respond as who you are choosing to become. Your life reflects that decision in each moment as well. The more you honor the relationship with your child as the guide to self-mastery that it is, the more you will no longer be able to recognize your life. For as you become the parent you wish yourself to be, that decision and consistent devotion will seep into all areas of your life; and life will no longer be able to reflect the same circumstances and beings that it once reflected back to you when you were creating your life moment to moment, based on conditioning. Your child has no desire to experience a limited life. As you expand, you aid more and more in the likelihood that they will not have to do the massive seeking, inner work, clearing, and healing that we have had to do.

PRACTICE #3

The Response-Only Method

When it comes to practices, I mentioned before that I enjoy simplicity. One of my favorite practices for parents is also one of the simplest yet most potent. This practice consists of dedicating a certain amount of time daily for responding only, and doing so as lovingly as feels available within the moments in that timeframe. When you commit to setting aside time to allow your child to just be themselves as much as possible in the moment, that is exercising your ability to stand in your sovereignty and allowing your child to bask in theirs. You are breaking the cycle of co-dependency. Even if only for a few hours at first, you are showing where you are in terms of your ability to not have your stability dependent on what your child does or does not do.

An example is choosing four hours to be responsive only towards your child - zero initiating whatsoever; and making it your only responsibility within that timeframe to respond to your child as lovingly as possible. It is a delicious practice that will both reveal a lot to you about your conditioning and deepen your knowing of the version of yourself you want most to embody. If your intention is solely to be as loving as possible during this practice you will greatly raise your vibration and be more in tune with your natural state of being and experience magic while interacting with your child. Whether you are familiar with the term vibration or not, you will feel amazing after this practice. You do not have to know anything at all about any spiritual or religious concepts to see the magic that is a result of this practice.

When our intention is to be our highest vision of ourselves as parents and we set aside time dedicated to the fulfillment of that vision in action, such as this response-only method, then over time your entire life starts to reflect that new way of being. You open yourself up to new ideas, opportunities, people, and more that could not be seen when you were more concerned with outcomes or anything else other than being the parent that you know you are at your core and that you prefer to be.

Most of us were raised to believe that effort is everything; and if that is a belief we hold, then as parents it can be hard to be present and actually available for our children because we are in a state of do, do, do, do, do. If you want to be a good parent and you associate being a good anything with effort, then it will be difficult to believe that to be that good parent you really do not "need" to do much more than to relax and just be with your child. When you are under the impression that constantly being on the move equates to productivity, then relaxing in the moment with your child can seem difficult and that is why this practice calls for you to start off by designating a timeframe to set the intention of only responding to your child with love - no doing the dishes, no vacuuming, no reading, no nothing - except being with your child and responding to them with love; and no you deciding what to do next...they get to initiate the next move in the moment. You just flow with it and take note of the moments where it is difficult to do so. Both the moments of resistance and total allowance experienced when utilizing this practice are journal worthy. The resistance is just where your intention is meeting your conditioning. Expand anyways. You came before your conditioning, therefore you are the stronger of the two.

So often we are focused on outcomes to the point where we are not present with others and instead are trying to figure out what we should do in the current moment or the next to ensure that our preferred outcome is the result. Most of us witnessed this way of living and it comes naturally to be in a state of survival.

Allowing things to be as they are, thus feeling relaxed in a way that many only feel on vacation, is amplified every time we give our children space to be themselves and make it our only responsibility to respond to them with love.

There is a life that you know deep down you are here to live and when you visualize it you smile and feel amazing inside. The version of you that is living that life is a much more expanded version than the version that reacts to the things you may currently react to in your experience. A good sign that more awesomeness is coming into your experience is when you start to react less and respond more in love. This shows your expansion and the more expanded you are the more space there is for more of the things to come into your life that play a role in you living a life that the higher version of you lives.

I AM stable

Our children came into this world as pure, unconditional love. They came in total awe of all that appeared before them. They did not come out of the womb with expectations. They did not come out of the womb needing you to validate them. They did not come out the womb begging for security. The behaviors that we take on as adults post-programming are not exhibited in infants, because they have not yet been conditioned.

When we were born, we would cry and whine but not to purposely manipulate. If our diaper needed to be changed, or if we were hungry or tired, we cried to express those things, since crying was one of the very few forms of communication available to us at that time. Not too long after that, we witnessed other people in our immediate experience carrying on in their day to day lives as if there was separation. I stated before that we came out of the womb without the concepts of you versus me or here versus there. We came out of the womb just in awe of everything that we saw. One day we look in the mirror and see a cute blob and, over time, we realize that others see us as that blob, separate from them, and we too take on the identity of that cute blob. If we were raised by those who were living in unity consciousness, knowing that we are all one, and if we were raised by caregivers who refrained from crying and whining about their circumstances but instead knew themselves to be the creators of their reality, then we would have continued to evolve without the belief that we have to give our power away in order to get our preferred outcome. Your power is in the form of your energy. For most of us, we grew up giving away our power by crying, complaining, and whining if something was not going our way; thus, giving our energy, attention, and power to others in those ways became a habit.

When we take on the belief that our outside circumstances dictate our state of being, then we act accordingly; and our actions reflect that belief. What that looks like as a parent is that the only way for us to be at peace is if our children are at peace; or the only way for us to be loving and sweet is if our children are first loving and sweet in their demeanor towards us. Life is constantly reflecting your state of being. Your children are no exception to that fact. When you respond to life how you prefer to respond to life, then everything in your life has no choice but to adjust accordingly. You be peaceful first, and let your child respond to that. You be kind first, regardless of your child's behavior, and let them respond to that.

Our children know what is possible first by what they see. As parents, we can show them that true stability is possible. True reliance and trust in oneself. When we operate as parents in a reactive manner, we do not show our children that anything other than emotional immaturity is what lies ahead in their future. We tend to say "Oh, that's normal. I am human after all," when it comes to reacting to others instead of choosing how to respond. No. It is not "normal." It is programming that has been accepted as normal. It is also a sign of emotional immaturity. To be so easily swayed by another's behavior shows instability. If we are unstable in this manner with our kids, it is a guarantee that we are unstable in that way with others in our lives as well. Once we stabilize in our being and respond to our child based on who we are choosing to be on purpose, that stability will seep into all other relationships and show others that such a stable way of being is not only possible but also very freeing and loving.

As parents, we want to be that rock for them and their emotions as they develop; and when we are not able to be, we feel resistance and oftentimes we place the blame of those resistant emotions on the child. When, in fact, we are being shown our instability and given the opportunity to act in alignment with who we want to be, instead of who we have been conditioned to be. Your child is not triggering you. They are showing you where you are and inviting you to level up. No matter how small the invitation, if you accept, you will positively alter all aspects of your life. You are worthy of all that comes with leveling up over and over again. Not just once. Not just a few times a week. No. You are worthy of all that comes with consistently leveling up.

We never stopped behaving the way we behaved as infants. That behavior evolved and became the collective's normal way of behaving. We just got older. Our bodies continued to grow but we never stopped believing that we had to give of our energy in exchange to get something we wanted. Every time you complain about your job, children, or anything else it is because deep down there is a belief that you must give your power away in order to get your preference. You are basically that infant that feels like they must cry for something outside of themselves to change. The infant's body evolved, and language was added unto the human; but the belief that one must give away their power in order to get what they want did not change.

How many generations must grow up watching mom and dad scream and cry to get what they want? Our children in the world now are not here to watch us behave in that way. They are here to witness the manifestation of what has already been asked for from the generations prior. It is time now for them to see what it looks like for us to be the change we want to see. This is going to look differently than how those before us behaved not just with parenting, but in all aspects of our lives. When you go from giving away your power and creating a life from a place of victimhood to standing solid in your power and being the parent you want to be, your actions and responses to your children and all other catalysts change as well.

This time around, we are not being called to repeat cycles of parenting that have been passed down over the years, but instead to transmute those cycles. Individually and collectively. Programming can be so thick that even when beings have recognized their own programming and healed, the version of themselves that arise from the ashes of said programming is not always easy to look at or understand through the eyes of those still heavily programmed. But one who has healed or continues to face themselves and is willing to do what is necessary to heal is not going to react the same to their children or in many other circumstances as those who have not looked within and are still expecting the change they seek to come externally first.

You are what your ancestors prayed for when they cried out for change. Your actions now in each moment impact the generations that come after you. We are being called to use each challenging moment with our children to change history. Not repeat it. Every time we react to anything, including our children, it is because we are still two months old and we feel we must complain and scream to get the result of our preference. That is the belief that is at the root of reacting to something outside of yourself to get it to change.

I AM *you*

We all come from the same Source which is why I say that we are all One. Regardless of what you believe in terms of religion or spirituality, there is one totality from which all human beings come. On the surface, we may appear to have differences, but as soon as you go beneath the surface you see similarities that unite us all. At the core of us all is the one source that we all are individuations of. If that is the case, but we are playing the game that we have to give our power away in order to get our preferred outcome, who exactly is it that we have to give to and who is it that we are receiving from, if in fact we are all one? If we all come from the same source, who am I begging to and who is giving to me? Because we are one and we all emerged from the same source and have that same source at the core of our being, we can stand in our power and choose in each moment to respond as the parents we wish to be and know that our children and anyone else will, over time, reflect that choice.

If you want to be a parent who loves your child unconditionally, speaks to them in a kind tone, plays with them, respects them, and honors them, etc., then be that now, trusting fully that in doing so it will be reflected back to you from your children. Waiting on your circumstances and others outside of you to be what and who you want them to be before you change yourself is a game that you will be playing until the end of this incarnation with little to no beneficial results, because life is a constant reflection of who you are being.

Before identifying with your body, it was not your screaming and crying that ensured that you were taken care of as an infant. Screaming and crying does not guarantee anything. You were taken care of because that is what was going to happen whether you screamed or not. You were just unable to talk as an infant. In this moment, now, you are being taken care of whether you scream and cry or not. You just know how to talk now. So if you are not aware that you are totally taken care of in this moment, you might be under the assumption that you need to form sentences with the emotion of need behind them in order to get something that you want. That is only an assumption. How has it worked out for you up until now to assume that you are not fully taken care of in this moment, and also that, in order to be, you must state your needs, complain, or whine? Your organs function and your blood circulate without the need for a single complaint or request to do so. It is conditioning alone over the years why we have forgotten that we can experience life with the same trust that we have for our body to do what it needs to do to regulate blood flow and keep organs functioning.

If it were true that you are not totally supported and taken care of in each moment and that screaming and crying would get you everything your heart desired, then it would also be true that the ones who do that the most would have a life that reflects that truth. An abundant life all due to screaming, bitching, and moaning. That, however, is not what we see to be the case.

If you believe that you must give your power away for something in life to be as you want it to be, then you are shooting yourself in the foot. Life will never reflect your preference if you operate from the belief that you must give away your power in order to get your preferred outcome. Maturity means ending that infantile way of operating and taking on the rewarding responsibility of creating life *on purpose* with your chosen response and actions. Otherwise, your relationship with your child will continue to be a tumultuous one. Furthermore, your child, as your guide, is giving you endless opportunities to see that belief for the nonsense that it is and to live the truth as the creator of your reality that you are. Statements such as "you are the creator of your reality" do not have to solely be a "new age" way of speaking. If really tuned in to such statements, it becomes clear that it is common sense. What you do, say, and think is a cause; and the effect of that cause is your life. Your choices. Your creations. Your responsibility.

MICHELLE BOWEN

I AM *healing*

Everything that your child's actions may bring up within you is being called forth to be seen and honored as a way of living that served you once, when you were unaware of your power as the creator of your life, and now no longer serves you. When we are unaware of our power as creators of our reality and have not yet taken on that responsibility, it is our unconscious behaviors that allow us to survive as humans on this planet. So, everything that our children bring up within us is to be honored for its attempt to aid in protection and survival and no longer needs to be ignored, suppressed, or judged. In honoring all that comes up when we interact with our children, we love that part of ourselves and love our total self unconditionally.

There is no logical nor beneficial reason to dwell in shame and guilt over how you may have parented throughout the years. Everyone is always doing the best they can from where they are, based on their programming. It is when you become aware of the conditioning that the catalysts may hit a little harder because you know better and have seen there are other ways, but continue to refuse to make higher choices. The past is gone. What you do now, as who you choose to be, is all that matters. You would not be the amazing individual you are without your past and that fact makes everything from your past beautiful. Total self-acceptance allows us to step into who we are becoming that much more powerfully. It gives us back more of our energy to place into the aligned responses we choose, instead of the reactivity we once defaulted to.

I AM *response-able*

There is energy flowing through your body which allows you to be alive. If you are playing the game of having to give of that energy to receive your preference, you are going to continue experiencing more of what you do not want instead of your preference. What is there to receive outside of you? What is anything outside of yourself going to give you? We are one. When we are not acknowledging that fact, we believe, think, and act like victims. Your children bring up all of the conditioning you are carrying around to be cleared, so that you both can live a life of freedom. They do not do this consciously. As children, their frequencies are high; and it is that frequency which they carry that brings up the conditioning to be seen, honored, and transcended. A child also holds space for all that work to be done. They are wonderful partners in this process.

If your child is behaving in a particular way that is bothering you and you react, the reaction is coming from a belief that you have to give your power away in order for your child to act how you prefer for them to act in this moment. That is also why it is very tiring. Each time we react it drains us of energy. People often associate having children with being a very tiresome task. It is tiring because you match your limited perception of your child's behavior instead of responding how you would prefer to respond.

You know that exhausted feeling you experience after yelling at your child in order to get your point across about what you would prefer them to be doing? That lethargic feeling afterwards that we blame them for in the end? That feeling that usually aligns with the concept, "Damn, why do I have to keep telling you this over and over again?" You feel that way because you do not need to keep telling them over and over again. You do not have to keep giving all that energy away in that manner. You believe that you do. You also witnessed and experienced that as a child and were conditioned to believe that is the way to behave despite it feeling like shit to do so. Like the infant you once were, you still believe you must scream and whine in order to get things accomplished. You will continue to do so if you believe you must.

It is such a strong belief; and even though you see that it is not serving you to continue doing so, you do it anyway. It is a belief that usually comes from experiencing and witnessing that same type of parenting and relationship style as a child, because your parents more than likely did not leave infancy in the ways previously described either. I do not mean this in a disrespectful manner. Emotional infancy is the way of most of our society. For the most part, our collective is reactive to their environment instead of response-able.

When reactive beings are in the presence of those who can respond despite circumstances, they are usually triggered. Shedding the conditioning that keeps you in a reactive state is the most loving thing we can do, because it benefits everyone we interact with. Even those who are triggered by you when you stand in your power and are not a slave to your circumstances are receiving the highest love from you, as you stand as the example of a being who has transcended the very programming that keeps them a slave to circumstances. You are also able to hold space for them in ways that you could not when you were reactive. You become childlike. Unconditionally loving. Your child is guiding you to the remembrance of this natural way of being. We do not have to give our power away any longer. We can keep it, stand firm in it, and allow the world to adjust accordingly.

I AM sovereign

The only difference between the undisturbed, childlike version of you and who you perceive yourself to be now is conditioning. A lot that disturbs you would not bother you if you were a child. You would not care at all or feel resistance regarding much of what you currently feel resistance towards if you were a child. You would be in awe most of the time throughout your day. There was a time when you were constantly in awe. No matter what appeared it wowed you; and the only disturbances were you being too tired, super hungry, or having a dirty diaper or a belly ache. Other than that, you were great. Great and in awe; and while predominately in that state, totally taken care of. Others who did not continue to live that way conditioned you to take things more seriously.

You were conditioned to think that you were not doing things right or that you were fucking up or that if you wanted to be "someone" you needed to do things in a way other than how you were doing it. This is all good news. The only thing preventing you from being calm, collected, and confident is conditioning. The only thing that is at the root of getting upset with your child and others over something seemingly big or small is: conditioning. The only thing in the way of knowing all is well and that you are awe-some without needing that fact validated by others and being dependent on the approval of others is: conditioning. The only thing in the way of being in awe all the time and seeing the constant evidence that you are totally taken care of is: conditioning. And if conditioning occurred after your arrival on the day you were born, then you are much more powerful than conditioning. Once you see that you are conditioned, then you get to choose moment to moment whether you react to life based on conditioning or respond how you would prefer to be. You have the choice because you are free to choose. How you choose to respond to situations determines the next slide in the movie that is your life. Because just like your Father...just like That which created you, you too are a creator.

I AM *love*

Whatever your form of discipline is now with your child, know that the following statements on discipline are not to judge you but instead an offering of a different perspective which some readers will share, and others may not. As with anything else, take what resonates and leave what does not.

Growing up as a child I got spankings. I was raised to believe that was normal and an okay way to discipline children. Because that was the belief that the elders in my family held, it was my reality as a child. As I got older and was in middle school, it was obvious that the majority of my peers' parents held that same belief. Watching movies and television series and being exposed to other viewpoints from other sources over time, I saw the enjoyment in some cultures to gather with family and friends and exchange stories, in jovial banter, of the times they were disciplined as children by means of violence. As I was growing up, I observed that it was a fun time for adults to go around the circle and share those experiences as though the experiences they had did not affect them negatively in anyway. As a child who was being spanked by the use of a loved one's hands or with a leather belt, it was interesting that such forms of discipline were the cause of laughter when being reminisced upon at family gatherings.

Even more interesting than the before-mentioned was the notion that violence in the form of discipline was, and is, done out of love. That is one hell of a mind fuck, is it not? Out of love. Love.

I am incredibly grateful for how I was raised, and I see a much bigger picture than what I was able to perceive as a child. My spankings were not in vain. I would not be who I am now if even one thing in the past were different. I am tremendously grateful for all I experienced as a child and all that I witnessed. Experience is our greatest teacher and the elders in my family were only doing what they experienced and witnessed as a child. Because I experienced violence as a form of discipline as a child, I had a reference point for what I did not want to do as a parent. Without that experiential reference point, physical violence with my own children may have been an option. It was not. Before my daughter's conception, I knew that I would not be spanking my child and I felt very strongly about it. This does not mean that I did not have programming to overcome regarding disciplining my daughter. I still lost my temper. Children feel you more than they hear you. You can tell a child you love them until you are blue in the face, but they learn what love is early on by who you are being when you say you love them. So even though I was not using physical violence with my child as a form of discipline, I still had my own conditioning to overcome and had to pull in the reigns on yelling and energetically expressing my anger and upset. I still had to realize that she was triggering me and I had to pay attention to what would arise in the moment, look at it, and then choose how to respond to my daughter as the parent I wanted to be, instead of reacting the way that I experienced as a child.

To be clear. Spankings. They are not right. They are not wrong. It is conditioned behavior. Children are still getting spankings when parents are triggered because the parents spanking them were spanked or worse when they were younger. Collectively we want reform, equality, and justice in many global arenas. Reform, equality, and justice in the home is going to have to come first before we see what we are capable of as a collective. Physical discipline is a thing of the past. Our children are the future and we are being called to treat them accordingly, regardless of if we were treated that way when we were children or not. In treating them as the divine beings they are, we heal the aspects of ourselves that are still wounded by our upbringing. In healing those aspects, we transform our entire lives.

It is especially important to note that there is no benefit to wallowing in guilt and shame of past occurrences. The fact that you are even slightly interested in another way of doing things regarding your child is huge for humanity. The forms of discipline and overall ways of parenting that have been passed down generation after generation need a revamping; and it starts individually at home, with each person that feels a call to switch up how they parent and then takes action accordingly. No one is at fault here. The old paradigm of parenting simply is no longer serving us, and we have seen that through our own experiences. We had to experience the old to feel compelled to create anew.

After I had my daughter, it did not take much time at all for me to get a better understanding of what was embedded in my subconscious from childhood that I had not looked at and had instead suppressed. If I wanted to be the parent I was becoming, I would have to let it all come up to the surface. There was no other way. Anything we suppress will come up at some point. It is inevitable. I had spent so much of my life suppressing so much that if I continued on that path it would not be good for my relationship with my daughter. I soon realized that all I had suppressed from childhood was not doing any good for my relationship with myself and all other aspects of my life.

There is so much out there about shadow work and healing the inner child. I remember when I first started to wake up, along with not wanting to learn about chakras and inner work, I also stayed away from shadow work and anything about healing the inner child. I skipped all those YouTube videos and never touched any of those books in Barnes and Noble. I did not want any part of it. It sounded like too much effort was involved. There was an Instagram page I loved, and the person who managed that page always had a hashtag in her work with the phrase "inner work" and it always fucked with me. I was starting to understand some of the best teachers to have ever taught self-realization and unity on an intellectual level, and could not fathom that there was more "work" to do.

I was only meant to ignore the inner work for so long; and it was the relationship with my child and my desire to become the parent I knew myself to be that created the space for the inner work to be done, using all that the relationship with my daughter brought to the surface. It was messy. It was not always easy. It is the most rewarding work I have ever done and continue to do. There is no end to expansion. Every time you expand you create a new edge. Every time you reach that edge and make a choice to become more of who you truly are you create another edge. There is no limit to love. There is no limit to expansion. There is no limit to your ability to choose to become more of you. The only limits are the ones that you create. A limited life is a life full of resistance and suffering. It is a limited way of living that allows us to continue to behave as though violence is the only way to get our children to behave how we want them to.

Limitations are what has been passed down from generation to generation. You who are reading this book and have made it this far without deciding not to continue further have decided to break that cycle and live a limitless life full of love and expansion and are choosing to pass that down to your children by way of example. Words do not teach. Experience does. Your example teaches your child more than any words you could ever speak. As you rise to the occasion in each moment to lead with love, your child sees in each moment that it can be done; and feels how amazing it is to be led with love and will not settle for less in their future.

Why do I refer to certain common forms of discipline as violence? Because it is violence. We all have a language we use collectively. We all call a spoon a spoon and a smile a smile. I do not use the word violence to judge. It simply is the word collectively used to label behavior involving physical force intended to hurt someone. It has just been normalized by society. It affects a child physically, emotionally, and mentally. It is violence and I do not say it to judge those who have used it as a form of discipline or who continue to. Calling something what it is, is not judgement. Referring to certain forms of discipline as violence seems judgmental to some because it is not something a lot who have either experienced it or are using on their children want to really acknowledge; because to acknowledge this causes parents to look within, and it would cause us to be responsible for finding other ways of being with our children at times when they are not being or doing what we prefer and that would stretch us. You would be stepping into the unknown and out of your comfort zone.

Regardless of how painful it is to constantly yell, scream, and hit our children, some continue to do it because it's the devil they know. It was done to us and it is what their peers do to their kids. It also gets the kids to be quiet and sit still effectively. It is also much faster than reading and researching other ways of being in those moments that are more loving. So most justify their behavior by any means to make it seem like it is not violence. If we look within and question what we experienced as a child and are passing on to our children as acceptable behavior, then we might actually see some things that could use adjusting, not just in the way we discipline but in many other aspects of our lives. This is the work I tried to avoid for so long. Looking within is not easy and is life changing. Looking within has tremendous effects on the life that one lives. When a parent starts to look at the fact that they do not feel good when they discipline in the ways their parents disciplined them, they start to see the programming. For some parents, this is their first time noticing that they are programmed. When a child triggers a parent and the parent, who knows deep down they love their child so much and would never want to hurt them, hits the child, and regrets it later, they make one of two choices after a while. They question their actions which leads them on a path that those before them did not take, or they continue passing that programming on to their child.

PRACTICE #4

The Smile Method

I want to invite you to smile for no reason when playing with your child. This practice is simple yet profound when practiced daily for specifically dedicated periods of time, and then eventually multiple times throughout the day. I want to invite you to smile with the intention to bring the joy that smile brings to your child and to witness the mirroring effect you have on your environment. When we practice smiling often when in the presence of our children, they feel that energetically as happiness, safety, acceptance, and love. My daughter would even say, "Now, that's the smile I like!" They feel all the vibes that we give off. All of them.

How do you want your child to feel? Realize that the only reason you want your child to feel the things you do such as happiness, joy, love, stability, and more is because that is what you want for yourself. Give it to yourself so you can have it to give to your child. Any practice mentioned here is just as much for you as it is for them.

You are impacted energetically by the practice first before anyone else. So, the practice is not so much to smile for no reason. You are indeed placing an intention upon it which is to smile often to give the joy that a smile brings to your child. Smile as often as you can when you are interacting with your children and watch the beauty that unfolds in your relationship with them and in all aspects of your life.

I AM *waking up*

Having a child is a call to wake the fuck up. It is a call to see the programming that one may not have seen roaming the world without child. For years we have parented our children as though they are to be controlled; and when you attempt to choose love and acknowledging your child's sovereignty over control, you may experience no longer getting validated by your peers. So, some tend to backslide into old programming when around family and friends to feel validated.

Over time, the reward that comes with leading with love outweighs the false benefits of validation and control. Every single destruction to one's reality that comes with enlightenment comes to the parent who chooses to lead with love, whether they are spiritual or not. Even if a parent has never heard of enlightenment or any other religious or spiritual reference, the path of a parent who feels called to lead their child with love instead of conditioning is a path of awakening; and it benefits not only the parent and child, but the collective as a whole.

Having a child is much deeper than just becoming a parent. You are directly impacting the next generation and the entire world with how you choose to parent your little ones. As you honor who you know yourself to be and live in the integrity of that knowing, your deeds, words, and thoughts align, and you become the living example of unconditional love in a way that only you can express.

I AM not a bully

As a child in middle school, I was severely bullied. The children who did this bullying did not know my grandmother was dying of cancer at the time, along with other things occurring in my life. Most bullies are clueless of what those they are projecting their pain onto are going through. That is understandable when you learn what the ones labeled "bully" are dealing with in their lives as well. I am in no way excusing bully-like behavior. I do want to point out that when children are spoken to at home as less than and hit by the ones that brought them into this world, with no ability to defend themselves, all of that anger and rage and pain will not stay suppressed for long. The things we see in this world that tear us to pieces when witnessed are symptoms of a much more deeply rooted cause.

As I grew up, I found that the kids at school that were bullying and constantly getting into fights with other children all had one thing in common. They were all being bullied at home by their parents, to varying degrees. In some cultures, it is normal to speak to your child harshly and to beat them. So, to call it bullying is inaccurate to many in describing what many families believe to be good parenting. I call any form of physical contact with the intention to alter or show discontent with another's behavior violence. It is something that, in most states, if done to a significant other, comes with judicial consequences for both parties, even if only one was violent. Over the years, domestic violence laws have become stricter. However, when it comes to children, the violence is looked upon as discipline; and some people use doctrines to support this conditioned behavior coupled with a splash of zero self-control. It was interesting to witness my own lack of self-control and massive conditioning as my child was growing up. It was very eye opening and I knew that if I did not make it a priority to be aware of my conditioning and course correct through aligned action, I would remain reactive to my child instead of lovingly responsive. As I got older and heard some of my peers' stories, I found that some were being abused on levels that is not necessary to explain here. Furthermore, as I got older, I was able to hear more details on the generational violence that occurred many years prior to my own birth.

The abuse that my parents, grandparents, and great- grandparents endured as a means of discipline was intense to say the very least. Generation after generation of abuse, both verbal and physical. The abuse that the generations before mine endured as a means of discipline makes spanking look like nothing, but it is not *nothing*. It is just a less turbulent form of violence than what was experienced by previous generations. Furthermore, violence is not just about hitting. When we really get to the root of why we do things and the resistance we feel when we take certain actions, we see that any action we take in order to control another is violent, in comparison with the bliss and unalloyed happiness that is available within each moment. Violence is not always physical. Generation after generation, and it all stops with you.

It all served a purpose. A lot of our behaviors are based on survival that stems from as far back as one can trace their lineage. However, we are moving out of a lengthy period of survival-based living into a period of love-based living. In this new paradigm, we honor and thank the past for showing us beliefs that served us when survival was key, and we let go of those beliefs since they no longer serve us. This is not a condemnation of those who have disciplined their children as they were conditioned to. This is bringing awareness to a way that is no longer serving humanity and shedding light on the fact that if something does not bring you joy, including how you discipline your child, then there are other ways; and you have every right to utilize whatever method feels best for you, and to witness the massive impact doing so has on your relationship with your child and the relationship with yourself. The relationship you have with yourself sets the tone for the relationship you have with all aspects of life. Your child is guiding you to a more evolved relationship with all of life.

I AM *respectful*

Can you respect your child as the adult that they are becoming? At the age of two, four, six and beyond...can you respect your child as the adult that they are evolving into before they are the age that society considers an adult? For so long, children have been perceived to be less than and treated as such. Those who treat their relationship with their children as a partnership can often be looked upon by the majority as irresponsible and naïve, until one day the majority sees this to be one of the most beneficial things we as parents can do to raise emotionally healthy and autonomous adults. When a child's sovereignty is not acknowledged for a lengthy period, co-dependency is a result. A co-dependent child is all that can come of a relationship where the parent acts from a place of being higher than the child. That type of relay is embedded in the subconscious of the child and acted out in all relationships, until the child becomes aware of that programming.

Once aware of any conditioning, one can take their power back and live life without validation from the very parents who they once needed to check in with before they made any life decision. When one no longer needs to be validated by their parents, they are easily able to live life with a sense of more freedom and self-confidence. When we parent our children as though they have no say in any matter and are just there to listen and follow our instructions, we set them up for a tough road ahead. A road travelled where they do not trust themselves. That type of conditioning is what has them wanting to be free when they are able to leave the house, but then simultaneously needing their parents more than ever due to lack of self-trust, self-respect, and self-confidence. Furthermore, when children lack self-love, trust, and confidence, they tend to seek that validation from peers; and seeking validation and love from anyone outside of ourselves never ends well, because no human alive is ever here to validate anyone other than themselves one hundred percent of the time. It can be a long road for some of us to discover that no external validation can ever give us the satisfaction we are seeking.

When, as parents, we allow our children to be who they are, it allows them to be confident in just being who they are with others. Allowing our children to be who they are can be triggering, because most of us were not allowed to just be. Most of us were raised by parents who were not allowed to be; therefore, it was not something that came easy for them to allow, due to conditioning. The way a parent should be, in your parents' estimation, is the way they themselves attempted to be based on how their own parents parented.

I have witnessed some of the most amazing expressions from my child when I was triggered and refrained from reacting. Doing so has allowed me to go beyond my conditioning and, in that expansion, allow my child to express more of her true self. I limit my ability to experience my child and her brilliance when I react based on conditioning. When you treat your child as an equal, as much as you can, considering they are indeed children and need to be looked after, then you are creating an environment for the child that allows them to trust, love, and respect themselves. You create an environment that does not foster a sense of inferiority within the child. The environment co-created within the home of the child is what the child takes out into the world. The environment created in the home has little to do with material things acquired and the type of home the child lives in, but instead has everything to do with where the inhabitants of the home are coming from in their moment to moment interactions.

When we come from love, freedom, compassion, and respect and acknowledge those virtues in the other members of our home regardless of their age, that becomes the environment that allows a child to be themselves and thrive. In allowing a child to be themselves, it cultivates self-confidence; and the child takes that out into the world and spreads those virtues with confidence and without need for recognition or reward. They are just being who they are, unrestricted. It is easier for a child to do that when they can be exactly who they are at home, instead of who our conditioning tells us they are supposed to be.

I AM *worthy*

It is essential that I acknowledge that you cannot get this wrong. You cannot fail your child. You cannot fail yourself. You are a creator in that where you come from and the actions you take create the reality that you experience. You can change it up anytime. Your choices. Your creations. Your responsibility. Each now moment offers you the chance to embody who you are here to be. You are here to be yourself.

Being yourself will always feel good. That is how you know you are being yourself with your child. You feel good. If any action with your child feels bad you can bet that you are not being yourself. Now this may seem irresponsible to many but that is because we have been conditioned to think that sometimes we are just going to have to do things that feel bad, especially when it comes to raising children. That is not true, and I honestly do not know why we listen to people who are not living life in a way that we would enjoy. If I want to be a millionaire, I really prefer to get tips from a millionaire or, at minimum, someone who was raised by one and is on the way to millionaire status themselves. If I want to have a healthy relationship with my significant other, I would like tips from a healthy and happy couple.

So often we take our advice from people who are regurgitating what they were told, but who are not at all experiencing the aspect of life they are speaking on in a way we would like to. I will say again that a particularly good way to know if you are being yourself with your child is if you are feeling good. Try it. The next time you are feeling angry or irritated with your child, immediately do something that lifts your spirits and then go respond to your child once you are feeling good. Whatever that response is, it will be more *you* than the reaction would have been while you were angry or irritated. I will take it a step further to say that you have not been angry or irritated your entire life. Anger and irritation did not come out of your mother's womb when you were born. You did. Anger and irritation come and go like the clouds. You remain. To give in to those fleeting emotions are leakages. What leaks? Your power. Your energy. That which would be better invested in loving yourself and others.

When you make a list of everything you want and every virtue that you want to embody in your day to day interactions, and when you imagine yourself as the person you wish to be, know that you are already that person right now; and the only thing stopping you from seeing evidence of that in the physical is you allowing conditioning to be stronger than your ability to embody that version of you in this moment. Your child is guiding you to the life of your preference and brings up beliefs that needs to be cleared. The clearing does not have to be some long, drawn out process. A simple dedication to responding, in the moments you are triggered with your child, in the way that the version you know yourself to be would respond clears conditioning. Calling out your conditioned reactions as the programming that it is aids in your healing and allows the space for the unconditionally loving parent you truly are to emerge and respond to your child instead. When you respond consistently as the version of you who you know and prefer yourself to be, instead of who your conditioning tells you to react as, you keep the momentum flowing of that higher version of yourself.

Everything you have ever wanted is on a timeline of a version of you who acts like the person who has those things. This is a blessing because if you were not yet being that version you would not be able to handle the responsibility that comes with all that you want. Wanting something does not mean that you will know what to do with it when you get it. Being that version first, with what is available to you now, ensures that when you do receive what you want, it is natural for you to take on all that comes with what you have received.

The life of a parent who genuinely loves their children and responds to them in each moment, while also loving themselves unconditionally, is rich, abundant, magical, miraculous, joyful, radiant, and full of surprises. Life cannot be any other way when you have made the decision to transcend your conditioning, thus leveling up your frequency and co-creating with your child. The creations from such a pair as parent and child are beyond your wildest imagination; and is available to you and everyone else who chooses to be who they *are* over who they have been conditioned to be, whether they have a child or not. The version of you that is a loving parent living a life that a genuine unconditionally loving parent lives is on the timeline where you are first being an unconditionally loving parent. You do not attain the lifestyle before first being that version of yourself.

I AM *devoted*

This can be quite simple. It can be as simple as recognizing when you are doing something that does not feel good and then noting that the only reason you continue to do it is conditioning. It can be as simple as yelling at your child and, instead of beating yourself up about it, asking yourself lovingly, "Why did I just react in that way?" and seeing that it was solely due to conditioning, then making a loving pact with yourself to respond in that situation next time as the version of yourself you prefer to be; and then continuing on in the present moment as the version you wish to be, without regret for what was just done due to conditioning. Ultimately, it gets easier the more you practice.

The more you commit to utilizing practices in place of reacting, the easier responding instead of reacting gets. I assure you that you will be given another situation almost identical to the one that triggered you, so you can play the game how you want to play it instead of how you have been conditioned to play it. I often refer to those triggering moments as portals. Those moments are full of so much potent energy that has been built up to the point of there being a type of threshold. It is as if those triggering moments are a glass ceiling; and each time you respond as you prefer yourself to be, you break that glass ceiling and expand into a larger and more loving version of yourself. It is as though in those triggering moments, there is a portal opening that you are going to go through one way or another; but the question is, on what timeline are you going to come out on the other side of this triggering situation? Are you going to move further along the timeline of being a slave to your conditioning and allowing circumstances to dictate your state of being? Or are you going to go through that portal and pop out further along the timeline of the version of yourself that you imagine yourself to be, thus bringing that version into physical form by being that version in the present moment and causing others to confirm that actualization, by responding to you as that chosen version?

You have created a child and, conditioned or not, the relationship you foster between you and your child is up to you regardless of conditioning. You have all the power to overcome your conditioning and it only costs you the choices you make in each moment. We can read and learn from others' experiences; however, everything will always boil down to the choices we are making in each moment. Our conditioning is a powerful tool because without it, how would we know our preference? How would we know the type of parent we want to be if we had not experienced or witnessed the parenting we do not want to embody? Our conditioning is an asset and, used properly, propels us further along the timeline of our preference every time it shows itself in any form and we choose to respond with love instead of reacting.

WE ARE *one*

At our very core we are all connected by that which we are each an individuation of. When we act from a place of separation, we feel fear, insecurity, and the need to survive and create a collective that has a theme of "survival of the fittest." Anything separate from you could hurt you; therefore, when you perceive all others as separate from yourself you act as though there is something outside of you to control or fear. Due to perceiving all outside of you as separate from yourself, you also tend to care for some more than others. Just as you treat some as though you have something to fear or control, you will treat others you place on a pedestal as though you need their validation. How we respond to others in our lives is a direct reflection of our ability to see the interconnectedness of all human beings.

Our relationship with our children is no exception to that. In each response, we are either being an example of unity consciousness or we are furthering our belief in separation. When those external to you are viewed as separate from you there is a constant war going on within; an instability and constant swaying due to fear, the need to control, the need for security, and the need for validation. The only way to treat each individuation of source that is in your immediate environment with the same love, generosity, compassion, and respect is to see the connectedness and that they are an individuation of what you yourself also are an extension of. When you view others as yourself and treat others as you wish to be treated, then we are being the love we wish to see in the world. One does not have to be self-realized to begin the journey of truly treating others the way they want to be treated in each moment.

When your child does anything that triggers you and you pause and respond the exact way you would want your parent to respond to you, as a child, in that moment, you expand in love and offer that love to your child and deepen that love within yourself and you feel that expansion in love. It is palpable. The more you expand in that way the more you cannot imagine taking those contrasting moments for granted. That is where the gold is. In loving where it does not feel natural in the moment to do so.

Our children are calling that superpower forth. There is a high that cannot be explained in words that comes from such a simple offering as treating your child moment to moment as you would want to be treated if you were them. It is a life-changing practice and one that inevitably seeps into all relationships in your life. Your external reality shifts drastically when the golden rule is put into practice with your children. The way we have been conditioned as a collective in regards to parenting has no room for the golden rule, because that conditioning sees children as less than; and in order to treat your child as you would like to be treated, you will have to see them as your equal and not as a being that is less than yourself. Your child came into this world through you but is not yours. Your child is as free as you are and there is much resistance when they are treated otherwise. You are only capable to see your child as free to the degree that you know yourself as free. Due to many years of conditioning, you may not have an easy time at living life as the free being that you are.

Practicing seeing your child as free and allowing them the space to be themselves uninhibited sets you free at the same time. Without the resistance felt in moments that a child's sovereignty is not acknowledged, we would not see the moments that we need to course correct with love so that we are on the trajectory created by our higher selves. Resistance is a call for more of you. For more love from you. It is a moment when you want to get your preference out of a person or situation, but would benefit tremendously by giving instead. Giving your allowance, your kindness, your patience, your love, your understanding, or your compassion.

When I was starting to wake up, everything I just mentioned was being practiced on everyone other than my child initially. I cannot explain why exactly, as it was not done on purpose. My child was an infant when I was still choosing to believe that understanding concepts from my teachers was enough. It was a bit later in her development that I honored application over consumption. I went into motherhood with a deeply rooted belief that parenthood was a hindrance to my realization and each time I was triggered in my relationship with my child, instead of utilizing that trigger to see what it was bringing to the surface, I looked at that moment as something further proving parenthood to be a hindrance to my realization.

I found it much easier to practice unity consciousness with everyone except my guide. I was on my path and my guide was staring me right in my face and I was looking everywhere else, because everywhere else was more comfortable. There is no expansion in comfort. Which is why my greatest expansion continues to come with how I interact with my child.

Our children are fresh out of the depths from which we came; and if we surrender to what they are bringing up within us and act in alignment with the highest version of ourselves that they are calling forth, we can actualize our highest version of ourselves in this world and give them an actual example of what they are capable of in this plane of existence. When I started to clearly see the potency of the relationship between me and my child, what she was teaching me, I was able to be the change I wished to see in the world. It started with taking a good look at all she was assisting me in bringing to the surface, and then seeing even more deeply how we are one and acting from that knowing. Consumption of information and teachings is a particularly good beginning; however, application in daily life with those in your immediate environment is a whole new ball game.

Whether you are reading this book and are spiritual or religious or just a parent with no type of interest in seeing a bigger picture than being a human on the planet, I ask you, even if the notion that we are all one seems like utter bullshit to you, what harm is done in acting accordingly? If when I say that we are all one you do not feel there is any real proof or if it is so far removed from the doctrines that you follow, what harm comes from coming from that place of oneness in your daily lives and when interacting with those in your immediate environment?

When it comes to parenting, it is really as simple as realizing that you and your child are in a divine partnership; and if you live by the golden rule, your life will change in ways you have not yet imagined and in some ways that you have. Are you willing to treat your child as you want to be treated? Furthermore, can you see that how you treat your child reflects how you treat yourself?

This realization can take us down a rabbit hole of immense focus on the why and the how regarding us internally neglecting ourselves. I tell you that healing can and will come from a change of action. A change of being. A decision is all that must be made in each moment; and with that decision comes both healing and actualization of who you prefer to be, and the relationship with your child that you prefer to have.

Are you willing to treat your child the way you would want to be treated if you were them? When they are screaming, whining, complaining, or yelling, can you set your conditioned reaction aside by going beyond it and see that they are expressing what is within them, and that it has nothing to do with you or whatever it may seem it has to do with in the physical realm, and instead go beyond all of that and express the love within yourself anyways? Can you see that when your child is expressing joy and happiness in ways that trigger you it is a time for you to expand beyond your comfort zone regarding the ways in which you have been conditioned are okay for the expression of happiness and joy? Can you accept their expression of joy and happiness and go beyond your conditioned response to it and, instead, respond in the way you prefer in that moment…even if that does not look like joining in on the expression, but instead doing what may have never been done for you as a child and just simply allowing them to express all of that love, light, joy, and happiness? Can you see that, like yourself, children have glass ceilings in regards to expansion and that as you rise to the occasion and be the version of yourself you know yourself to be and continue to break through glass ceiling after glass ceiling, your child has to meet their thresholds and break through as well? As you rise, so do they. It can be no other way. In your self-initiated evolution of self, you are taking your child with you. They are not getting left behind.

PRACTICE #5

The Call-Out Method

Another very potent practice to do with your child is to call yourself out when you are noticing the programming. You can set aside time to do this when being with your child or make it an ongoing practice throughout your days. It is a very loving practice and not judgmental at all. We are simply calling the conditioning out amid witnessing it, therefore, putting a halt to acting on whatever behaviors usually result by identifying with the conditioning. What this may look like in real time is your child having a genuinely good time alone in the living room jumping on the couches, and a thought coming up that they should not be doing that. Instead of acting on that thought, just witness it and even go as far as to call it out by stating aloud that you are seeing the programming.

This is just an example, but when applied each time you encounter resistance, this practice is very powerful as it stops you in your conditioned tracks and allows for more of who you really are to shine through and changes the trajectory of the moment, because you are not acting from conditioning anytime you bring your awareness to the conditioning. What we tend to believe our children should or should not be doing is usually what was expected of us based on our parents and society's conditioning. A lot of times the resistance with your children is simply because deep down you do not care if your super cute and sweet child is jumping on the couch. Deep down there is a part of you that finds it cute and is happy that they are happy and finding such joy in doing something so simple as jumping on a couch. When you bring awareness to your thoughts in moments of resistance such as when you are about to react based on what a thought says your child "should" or "should not" be doing, you give all the space needed to see how you truly view what your child is doing. Often you will find yourself smiling and finding magic in moments that used to bring forth a conditioned reaction. It does not take long to see that our "shoulds" are programs. Who exactly determined what should or should not be happening in any moment? Why exactly should your child not be jumping on the couch? No matter how logical one tries to get you will feel the realization quickly within that nothing is ever as big of a deal as our conditioning makes it seem. It can seem as if not saying "stop jumping on the couch" means they will continue to, but that is not how this works.

What triggers you is bringing up suppressed emotions to be felt, accepted, and released and giving you an option to choose to feel good regardless of what you are seeing before you or to be a slave to conditions. In truth, whatever causes the trigger is irrelevant in that moment, and all that is required is your willingness to be with whatever came up within you and to allow it space to be released. Afterwards, if it is relevant, you can respond to your child or whatever triggered you or not respond. Often, after a moment of introspection, we find that whatever triggered us is not even worth acknowledging. However, if you choose to respond afterwards it will be a lot less reactively charged and more loving due to your awareness and intentionally being with what arose within you when triggered.

I AM *infinite*

In each moment in time, there are infinite possibilities. There are infinite potentials available to you regarding how you choose to be in each moment. There are infinite timelines in each moment that are made up of those infinite potentials that you choose in each moment. The timeline that has everything you want, and more, is made up of you continuously choosing to be who you want to be in each moment.

The resistance you feel is an indication of a point in time where you can either continue on a timeline that is not in alignment with the higher version of yourself, or you can level up and be that version in that moment. When this is your way of life, the situations that you once dreaded become your favorite moments in time. You start to look forward to when your child does something that triggers you and you see it as the greatest opportunity for expansion and you take that opportunity on with a fucking smile, and you look forward to the next and the next and the next; and even when life starts to reflect your expansion, you continue to look forward to the next opportunity for expansion.

It is a good thing you start to see those contrasting moments for the gold that they are because, until the day you take your last breath, you will forever be expanding; therefore, you will always come face to face with moments where you are breaking through yet another glass ceiling. There is no end to your expansion. You are always just beginning and forever in a state of becoming. "Oh, but when will it be done!? When will my child be done doing things that stretch me?" Never. You are forever expanding. You are always being called to step into more of your *Self*. Be thankful that it is your child that came from your womb pulling you through the eye of the needle. Take a moment to feel into who and what could be calling you forth to more of your *self*. You are blessed that it is your child.

So, when you and your child's relationship is feeling better than ever before, do not ever get too comfortable and label the journey as complete, because more expansion is on the way. So often on this journey we can begin to experience the rewards of our choosing aligned action continuously, and we can view moments of resistance with our children as a negative thing, as though we are not doing good enough in being who we know ourselves to be. That is nothing more than a thought. What is really happening is that you are being called to more expansion. Nothing more. Nothing less.

The belief that there is a destination on this journey of expansion is the foundation of the repeated thoughts that are along the lines of us needing to have already conquered a certain situation. There is nothing to conquer; if anything, there is a constant conquering. There is a constant going beyond conditioning. There is a constant becoming. You are never going to be done expanding. You are going to forever continue to show yourself, through aligned action with your child, who you really are and what you are truly capable of.

I AM *trusting my self*

The relationships that were based on who you are *not* will either fade away or be healed, in the areas where healing is called for, and amplified when you honor and act aligned with who you know yourself to be. When you start to treat your child as you wish to be treated, and as you act in alignment with who you want to be in ways that are less resistant and more true to who you are choosing to become in each moment, you will face opposition with those who are not consciously undertaking such an endeavor in their own lives. This again is good news. It is a sign that you are staying the course you are paving for yourself and not settling for what is more commonly accepted. It is here that we are called to put our preference before validation of others.

When family members, peers, and strangers view your preferred ways of being as wrong or not the way a parent should be, are you willing to see that their views are based solely on their conditioning and have compassion for them while standing your ground and continuing to honor your child's sovereignty and your own? I say compassion and not pity because how we view the world prior to choosing how we wish to view the world is based on how we were conditioned to view the world. One may have been raised by a parent who went to church three out of seven days a week, and read the bible or whichever book relates to their religion to all of their children every night; but if that same parent did not embody the virtues and teachings taught to them, then what they did embody was also a part of their children's conditioning. We were all conditioned and it is through the lens of that conditioning that we tend to see and judge the world. Compassion comes in when we realize that we get to choose how we view the world and that option is available to all; but some may not be partaking in that option due to conditioning, and their conditioning is no reason to love them any less. We were too completely identified with our own conditioning. We don't wake up and then judge everyone else.

Everyone's coming home. There are infinite ways each walk home will be experienced. But everyone's coming. Truly, no one ever left. Those who do not view how you are being as the "right" way are not themselves "wrong." They are simply seeing things from their level of perception. Pitying others is to say that they are wrong, and it is a shame. No one is wrong. Everyone is right as per their level of perception. Unconditional love is loving others regardless of where they are on their journey. Unconditional love is allowing others to be as they are.

As you continue on the journey of acknowledging your child as your guide, the opposition faced is always a question to you as to whether those in opposition's validation is more important to you than expanding more into the unconditional loving being that you are becoming. Are those tiny hits of validation from others that you receive when you act in ways that validate how they believe one should act worth not becoming the parent you wish yourself to be? Once you make a decision to put who you are becoming before the validation of others, some who have been in your life will inevitably fall off; and space will be made for those who are in alignment with who you are becoming to come forward.

I AM *free*

Can you see that there is no need to judge yourself any longer? Can you see that because the reason we react in certain ways is due to conditioning that we need not judge ourselves, but are instead redeemed in that realization? There is a constant stream of energy flowing within you and self-judgement no longer must play a part in causing any resistance in that flow. When you react or behave in a way that reflects how you used to be, based on conditioning, it is okay. The further along you go on this journey, the more sensitive you will be to those moments that are so far removed from who you both know and prefer yourself to be.

Those moments are going to stand out much more than ever before, and that is a huge blessing. For there was a time when you never once even paused to reflect on your behavior, but were completely identified with being solely how you have been conditioned to be in the area of parenting. The fact that you recognize when you are not acting in alignment with who you know yourself to be shows tremendous growth and acceleration. If you can take a moment to love yourself for being at that point where you see the behavior and choose to get back in alignment with your preference, you not only get back on track with the constant stream of energy flowing within, you also accelerate your journey by not staying stuck where you may have once stayed stuck energetically by beating yourself up for reacting a certain way towards your child. You also teach your child through your example the version of you that is dominant. You have made your preferred state of being dominant regardless of if you react towards your child as you may have in the past, based on conditioning. That conditioned reaction is no longer your dominant way of being. You are in human form and, since that is the case, unconditional love is all that is necessary towards yourself in moments that once produced bouts of self-criticism or judgement. There is no one to blame. We are evolving and, in doing so, consciously leveling up the parenting playing field.

I AM *aware*

Ultimately, as parents, we are embarking on a path of allowance. Can you allow your child to be who they are unapologetically? Can you see that our inability to allow our child to be who they are is where there is resistance? Can you see that a lot of the resistance our parents felt while raising us was due to their inability to allow us to be who we were? Can you see that the only reason we do not allow our children to be who they are is conditioning? It is conditional love that is okay in the moment with our child, so long as they are acting in agreement with how we believe they should be acting. That is very limiting for a being that has infinite potential available to them in each moment. Over time, they will conform to limits in order to appease their caretakers and feel the love they receive when they act how their parents prefer; but because it is limiting and there is so much more available to them in terms of love and life as they get older, it is no wonder why they may evolve beyond those limitations which may not look anything at all like what the parents were expecting or wanting their child's evolution to look like. Your child can feel when who they truly are is not accepted.

At the root of everything I wanted in life, I found the desire to just be. When I realized I could be who

I truly am, unrestricted no matter what my circumstances, then life began to shift based on that alone. Just being. It was getting easier to just be with others who do the same; but sometimes, when with the majority, there was a sense of uneasiness about just being. Just resting as I am. I felt myriad things. Awkward. Anxious, because I was sensing that something was expected of me by way of my actions or responses, as though I was not fulfilling an obligation on my part; or thinking that if I continue to just rest as I am, that I might lose something. I may lose the validation of others or make them uncomfortable; therefore, just being may not be a nice thing to do. Fuck that. Not much else nicer can be done. Bliss, love, joy, ecstasy, and more do not always look like what we have been made to believe. Thankfully. It would be exhausting if being happy twenty-four-seven meant always moving in some way or doing something. I did not have to wait until anyone got on board with my preference to be me unapologetically. I did not need to make sure I had my parents' or peers' validation to be me unapologetically. I did not have to have the car, house, or relationship of my dreams to be me unapologetically. All of that comes after you decide to be who you know yourself to be instead of who you have been conditioned to be.

As parents, we can allow our children to live that way as children; instead of them realizing they can be themselves fully much later in their lives. They can be allowed to be themselves now. What is extremely confusing to children is seeing their parents be one way when they are alone with them, and then another around other people. This confusion becomes normal human behavior over time and the children mimic it by also acting differently around different people. A lot of the things we do not want our children to do they picked up from us, but we do not realize that because we are not aware of our own programming. Our children are guiding us to our authenticity. The degree to which we can be authentic is the degree to which our children are comfortable doing the same.

I AM confident

Our child's being confident is a byproduct of allowance. When we allow our children to just be, they become extremely confident. Just as confident as you become when you expand further into your own authenticity. Even when we transition and our children are left here on Earth without the presence of our physical bodies, their confidence does not waver; because, while we were here with them, we gave them space to be themselves and, in doing so, let them know that they are worthy of self-expression no matter what it looks like. That allowance also showed them that they do not ever have to settle for anything less than being who they are.

Seen from a place of confidence, a problem is not a problem. Seen from a place of confidence, whatever behavior your child exhibits that brings up resistance within you is not ever the issue, but an invitation to more of who you are choosing to become. It is the next step, leading to what you have been asking for. When you take the invitation that resistance is generating and respond as who you want to be instead of who you have been conditioned to be, you are confidently choosing to become more of who you truly are. There is no becoming who you know yourself to be without confidence. You have never been dealt anything that you could not handle. And you never will be. Your ability to do or be anything is dependent on whether or not you know you can do or be anything. With alignment comes confidence. The two cannot be separate. The relationship with your children grants you many access points to your highest timeline. There are so many opportunities each day with your children to make a higher choice. The way you respond to life on average is what becomes easiest for your children to mimic as they develop.

As parents, if we allow our children to be themselves as much as possible, we can then love them for who they are and not who we want them to be. We only want our children to be something specific based on our conditioning. We can say we want this and that for our children because we love them, but who is to say that any other option available to them in life is not a great fit for them? The outcomes of our children's lives are not about us. Our child is not about us. How our children behave is not to be taken personally. Our child came through us and is here to create themselves based on who they are at their core. The same goes for you. You did not come here to be a replica of your parents. You came through them to be who you came here to be.

When we make the outcome of our children's lives about us, we are setting limits on limitless beings. Your child, like yourself, is pure potential.

When you recognize that you are creator of your reality and choose in each moment who you are becoming, you offer that same freedom to your child. It is when you remember your sovereignty that you are then able to be your child's guide. One in bondage to conditioning is never a guide or teacher to anyone. Children do not come out of the womb conditioned. They come out the womb sovereign. Therefore, if you are still operating based on conditioning, they are your guide. No matter how conditioned they are at a certain age, they are still more in tune with their sovereignty than a parent who still reacts based on years of conditioning and what others think. By using your relationship with your child as an entry point to healing conditioned patterns and becoming who you prefer to be as a parent, you remember your sovereignty.

When you get in the habit of allowing your child to express themselves unrestricted, you see so much more of who they are and can fall so much more in love with them. That habit of allowing deepens the unconditional love within yourself. When you practice allowance in this way with your children, it seeps into all aspects of your life and you are then able to love yourself and others unconditionally. You begin to never again want to settle for anything less in any relationship. Not allowing others to express themselves without judgement or condemnation is then seen as limiting, and you begin to see how it has only been you and your choices that has been the cause of living life in a limited way. It is no longer about our conditioning and becomes solely about whether in each moment we are going to choose to be limited or limitless in our response to life.

This does not happen overnight, but takes practice. The practice alone produces results quickly because we are making different choices, and different choices produce different results no matter how seemingly small.

We are only here for a short period of time. We owe it to ourselves to live our lives on our terms and to make decisions that we want to make, not decisions that we have been told are best to make. We owe it to ourselves to trust in ourselves and to create a life from that trust, instead of creating a life from a place of doubt.

I AM making the higher choice

I eventually also realized that every time I was feeling resistance with my child was precisely when I could open up and show unconditional love in those moments. Every time I was triggered by my child was an invitation to be more loving than I have ever been. Each moment we are triggered by someone is an opening to choose one of infinite loving ways to respond, as opposed to reacting in the resistant way we always have up until that moment. When I started to view those moments as invitations to remain open and choose to express more love, I started to feel more love than I have ever felt in my entire life; and this love was not dependent on anything outside of me. We begin to move with a knowing that external circumstances hold zero weight regarding how much love we feel inside.

I cannot fully describe the benefits of living with one's heart open and reinforcing that lifestyle in each moment by choosing love over conditioning. What we are discussing here is a path that is unique to each individual, and along that path is everything one wants in this life and more. I invested a lot of money on books and courses throughout the years; however, I eventually saw that I was consuming and not applying. As soon as one starts to, in the moment, apply even a fraction of a fraction of what is consumed, results are seen immediately in their life.

There was nothing at all wrong with my seeking and consuming. It was a divine part of my path and, during that time, I had to play out certain circumstances and gain the lessons learned in doing so; however, one of the biggest lessons learned is that there is no better time than now, and that the only time is now, to apply what has been recognized as beneficial.

This book is not to tell you how to parent. This book is not to tell you that you are doing anything right or wrong. I wrote this to offer my perspective on the matter. I have learned on my journey with my child that she is guiding me to a life of unconditional love. I wrote this because all of our children are guiding us on that path and there are not a lot of perspectives reflecting this to be the case; but, there will begin to be as we continue in this shift that is occurring on the planet.

I want you to know that you are never alone in wanting more for the relationship between you and your child, more than what you have witnessed in society or experienced in your own relationship with your parents. I want you to know that leading with love in all relationships can seem like an act of rebellion in the eyes of those around you who are not deeply feeling the pull to do the same. That is okay. You are not here to please others.

The highest version of you is so loving. The highest version of you does not judge but is discerning. The highest version of you is compassionate. The highest version of you is living the life of your dreams. Your child gives you opportunities daily to align to that path; and you and your child are worthy of that alignment and all that comes with it.

PRACTICE #6

The You-Are-Invited-to-The-Party Method

No matter what they are doing when you witness your child exhibiting behavior that shows they are elated, take that as an invitation to join them in their elation. Even if joining them in that joy is done while you continue to work or do whatever activity you were doing that may not have involved them. Your environment and those in it are always showing you evidence of your own vibration. Well, Michelle, if that is the case, then why does my child irritate me in those exact moments that you are speaking of? Because they have taken you to your tolerance threshold. Tolerance of what? Of how much of that high vibration you can handle.

When our child is exhibiting any behavior that shows that their vibration is elevated, that is a moment in time that is precious beyond measure. Any moment that your child is showing you that they are happy, joyous, relaxed, or in any elevated state that is the time to either let them remain there or join them. Doing anything else is a cue that we are reacting based on conditioning. We have a threshold, so to speak, of how much happiness we can take from our child. The degree to which your parents could tolerate you expressing your joy unfiltered in the infinite ways that may have manifested when you were a child is the degree to which it will be easy for you to allow your children to express themselves in that high vibrational state. Your child might be running all over the house, jumping on the sofas, rolling on the floor, singing very loudly, or any other myriad ways children love to express themselves and you will only be able to lovingly tolerate as much of that behavior as was tolerated from you lovingly by your parents or those who were influential in your childhood; and that is okay, because you are here to expand beyond those thresholds.

Once you have expanded beyond those thresholds, you will be called to expand even more. Even if before you have a child you envision yourself being completely and unconditionally accepting of your child's expression, there will be a threshold. Even if your threshold is beyond that of your parents, there will still be a threshold. There is never *not* a threshold because you are an infinite being in a body and you are always being called to expand beyond whatever illusory limits you are believing in. The moments of resistance with our children is where we are meeting our threshold. We are no longer in the comfort zone of what we have accepted in the form of our child's behavior. What is happening in these moments of resistance with your child is you being called to expand. To stretch. To grow.

Can you love more in this moment? Can you see that your child is happy and be happy about that in this moment? Can you see that your irritation with the moment is conditioning and choose to see what there is to be thankful for instead in this moment? Can you instead of contracting in this moment step into the unknown and respond in a way that you have never responded before, therefore literally changing you and your child's experience, and bringing newness into your lives in this moment? When we see the resistance as a call to step into the unknown and become more than what we have been allowing ourselves to be, we are no longer playing a victim to circumstance. We are choosing how it is going to be instead of letting limiting beliefs and conditioning dictate how it is going to be. Join in on the party.

I AM *authentic*

If you did not receive "it" as a child, it's going to be hard for you to give "it." It being the myriad loving qualities that are natural for you to radiate, unless disempowering mental chatter prevents doing so. Therein lies your work. This is the inner work that your child is guiding you to and allowing the space for aligned action, as the version of yourself you are here to embody. For it is only when you can authentically experience, for yourself, the qualities that were not exemplified by the adults in your environment as a child that you are able to radiate authentically those qualities to another. I say authentically because any quality can be feigned. Those of us who have experienced depression know all too well that we can smile our asses off while experiencing inner turmoil. That mask is heavy, but we can wear it so well. However, we cannot fool ourselves. Nor can we fool those who have done and continue to do the work. In order to experience authentically loving, uplifting, healthy relationships with others, we will first have to cultivate that relationship within. Treating others as you treat yourself is only beneficial to others if you treat yourself with love.

I AM home

You do not need to be fixed. You are not doing anything wrong. That realization is inevitable and the only real acceleration of that realization, which is essentially only brought about by GRACE, is your own unconditional love. That is the key. There is no code to crack. There is no secret that is available to others and not you. There is you loving yourself unconditionally, unequivocally. Accept everything that arises within you. See that you are not the conditioned thoughts that arise but the space in which the arising happens. The awareness of what arises.

You are becoming more than you have ever been before. It is happening. You can prolong realizing yourself as the love that you are, or you can use unconditionally loving and accepting yourself and all that arises moment to moment as you are to accelerate the becoming that is happening anyways. You are worthy of all that is on the path you are on. The more you love and accept all that arises within you as conditioning that once served you when you were not aware of your ability to choose infinite options in each moment, the more you being beyond all that arises becomes an unshakable knowing. Acceptance of all of you instead of suppression and rejection. The more you accept all of you, the more you can accept your child and others as they are.

Your child came out of the womb nothing less than confident. Children have no reason not to be confident; however, they must deal with conditioned adults who, due to their own lack of confidence, condition their children to doubt themselves. Your child is guiding you to get on their level. Children simply know that they exist and are naturally only just being. Unfiltered. That is confidence. A child is exuding their innate confidence until an adult attempts to hinder that divine self-expression or make it conform to however the adult was conditioned to believe that a well-behaved child is supposed to act.

Confidence. According to the dictionary, confidence means: the feeling or belief that one can rely on someone or something; or firm trust.

What is it then that a child is relying on at such an early age? They have firm trust in who they are. More than anything they have firm trust in the knowing that they are. Just being is enough for them until it is not. Just being is not enough for a child when they are conditioned to believe it is not enough. We carry that belief into adulthood until we wake up from that slumber and remember that just being is enough and that we can be confident again in just being. Your child is guiding you to see that there is a version of you that is more relaxed and accepting of them just being; and that version of you is also confident in just being yourself. Our resistance to our children is showing us the moments where we are not able to simply be. Our resistance to our children is showing us that if we allow them to be, we may see magic and experience love we have not yet experienced due to conditioned responses putting a cap on the amount of love we are able to express in that moment. Blow your own damn mind in those moments of resistances. Just be.

No reason is needed to be your highest self. No reason at all. You are worthy of being that version now and experiencing life as only that version of you can. When your child witnesses a life lived from a place of worthiness, confidence, and stability in being, you are then able to guide your child by showing how that love is able to be expressed in the world as an adult; which is what they are evolving into.

I AM *taking my power back*

It is quite easy to, at minimum, be the average of persons who raised you; until you become aware of your thoughts and behavior patterns, instead of identifying as them. When we are asleep and living life unconsciously, our job may be like our parents, our relationship dynamics may be like our parents, how we parent will be like how we were parented. Why? Because that is all we know until we remember that we can choose how to be in each moment. The moment we start to pause before speaking or acting, choose what we say and do, and make decisions based on our preference instead of what we experienced, we take our power back and are creating as we are meant to. The reason resistance arises when you attempt to be anything other than what you witnessed as a child or anything contrary to how you have been conditioned, is because when you are not operating from conditioning, you are in the unknown.

You never intimately saw the outcome of living a life of your preference, so when you opt to do so it is a bit terrifying. So much around you tells you that parenting the way you prefer is not the best way. There are books, religions, family members, and high-profile people who may say that a lot of your preferred way of being is wrong. So ultimately, it feels like that is what you are up against when you first embark on the journey of responding to and creating life on your terms solo, without those whose validation you once needed. That can be scary. It is terrifying just to realize that you are programmed to begin with, much less taking action outside of that programming; but it is the only way out of living the conditioned life, and you are fucking worth it. You have been worthy of living life how you choose since the moment you were born. Your worth was never something you have to earn, and never will be. An effective way, in the moment, to check yourself is to question if how you are behaving is in order to prove something. If you are ever speaking to your child, friend, significant other, family member, or anyone else in any way to prove yourself, then you are operating based on conditioning.

There will never be anything for you to prove. Ever. You did not come into this world to prove anything but to create based on who you are choosing to become. If you are acting in any way to prove something, you are operating based on conditioning. Your child is guiding you to a state of ease and allowance. You, in turn, are showing your child that it is possible to be an adult in this world while also living in a state of allowance, ease, trust, and self-confidence.

I AM *unconquerable*

What was slavery as we have been taught? There were "masters" who owned land and saw beings as their property. Those beings were known as slaves. Those slaves' livelihoods were dependent on their ability to do what their masters asked of them. Slaves were "safe" to a certain degree and not beaten harshly if they did what they were told, exactly how they were told to do it. This was a co-dependent relationship. All relationships where one must do anything to keep the other feeling how they want to feel is co-dependent. The master was not happy when the slave did not do as they were told, and the slave suffered when the master was not pleased. Both parties were slaves. The master may have appeared to have more freedom than the slave, but a slave he was, nonetheless, if he was swayed by the actions of another. You are a slave to anything that you think you can control or that you think you own.

Being a parent is no different. We can fool ourselves into thinking that there is a difference, but doing so does nothing for the parent or the child. When we treat our children as though we own them or in a way that undermines their sovereignty, we are creating a co-dependent dynamic. We are also being a slave to our child, which does not feel good; and resentment is the result of this resistance. The resistance with your child feels so potent because in those moments, you are a slave to your conditioning but project this onto your child; which is far removed from how you really want to treat your child. You are a slave to believing something outside of you needs to be different to feel okay in that moment. At your core you are not a slave. You are sovereign. You are free.

So because what you are truly at your core is a sovereign being, free of all cords and attachments, anytime you act otherwise you will feel it as a wakeup call telling you that you are a slave in that moment and have been up until that point, but are being shown it now in this moment with your child. When you take your power back in these moments with your child, you are breaking cycles of that co-dependent way of parenting. You are breaking cycles of that co-dependent way of being.

When you are not able to accept others, you can be sure that there are parts of you that you do not accept as well. The more you accept yourself the more you can accept others, and your acceptance of others is both powerful and transformative. The more you can just be and accept all that arises within you and not identify with the thoughts and emotions, the more you are able to allow all others to just be! Acceptance of yourself and others is equivalent to a permanent vacation! On vacations, one feels open and able to just go with the flow. On vacations, we are excited about random strangers we meet and open and receptive to those encounters and new experiences. Linear time flies by because you are not focused on time! You are just going with the flow because there is nothing but acceptance of whatever happens.

This is the life available to all each day of the week, whether on vacation or not, when one accepts oneself, others, and whatever arises in the moment and chooses to not be against anything that comes their way; but instead, they take what happens and co-create with it by choosing how they prefer to be and respond. Then no matter what happens outside of you, it cannot shake the stability within you due to your ability to accept whatever emotions and thoughts arise regarding the perceived circumstance. You are too stable within and why? All because you have accepted yourself and what arises for you in the moment. Everything that arises in the moment is for you. You are never a victim to what arises in the moment but instead are being asked how you would like to take what arises and create art with it. Your response to your children is artwork. Your response to all of life is your artwork. You are an artist.

Of course, what you are is beyond any label, but it is what you are that is creating through you. You are worthy of what you prefer to be. You are worthy and deserving of allowing the artwork of your preference to be created in your life. When you are able to accept every single thought and emotion that at one point in your life you suppressed, then nothing anyone outside of you does or says can shake you; because you are able to accept whatever arises.

Your openness to the moment is love. You give love when you are open to the moment and you can receive it because of that openness as well. Your child is open always and does not understand why anyone would be anything other than open. There really has never been a good reason to be closed. The only reason one is resistant is due to conditioning. Your child is guiding you back home. Your child is giving you many opportunities to choose allowance over conditioning.

I AM *here to play*

Your children are inviting you to play. When you feel like you cannot, it is time to do the work. It is at those times that we apply practices that align us back to our higher selves. Because, not only can you play, but playing is what you are here to do. The only thing preventing you from joining in on the fun ever, at any time, is your conditioning. The only reason we hold beliefs that what is happening here is serious business is because that is how we were raised. We were raised by parents, grandparents, societies, etc., that themselves believed that what is happening here on this planet is serious business and that there is such a thing as playing too much.

"Well, Michelle, if we are here to play then what is it with the programs, the one on one sessions, the speeches, the inner work, etc.?"

Why continue to suffer? Why not feel the bliss and unalloyed joy that is your true nature? Why continue to loop painful patterns with our partners and children? Why pass down a conditioned way of being to our children? Why not accelerate? Let's play the game the way we want our children to play it when we leave. If we can enjoy each moment and have compassion and love for all beings and ourselves and create a life from that love, joy, and bliss...why would we choose otherwise? Our children are guiding us home. Back to where we were before we took on the programming that was fed to us. Back to where we were curious and playful and did not let doubt, fear, or shame stop us from expressing ourselves. Back to where we were creative. Back to where we did not think about lack but only saw abundance everywhere we looked. Your child is your guide.

I AM *unconditional love incarnate*

Before having my daughter, I only ever imagined parenthood as a blissful time of me loving my child unconditionally. I only ever envisioned laughter, love, happiness, adventure, and a deep bond. This is indeed the relationship I have now and continue to cultivate, but it is not what I experienced until I saw clearly that I was often in a state of resistance regarding my child. I was unintentionally attempting to manipulate my experiences with my daughter every time that I was not present and intentional in my state of being and the frequency that I was broadcasting in the moment. I was more concerned with what I believed I should be receiving from my child in the moment. I had given away all my power and I did not get it back until I was more concerned in each moment with my child with what I was giving instead of what I was receiving from her. That was and is a game changer. To be more concerned with the energy with which we are impressing upon another instead of how or what they are doing.

What I impress energetically upon my environment has a direct impact on the feedback I receive. This is also why taking aligned action with your child is not always sufficient. The energy from which you take that action matters. In order for the action to be aligned how you feel while taking the action needs to match the feeling you wish to impress upon your child. Are you pissed but determined to implement a practice such as hugging your child when resistance is felt? Take a moment and breathe, smile, and then act. With all practices mentioned in this book, or if we are ever to meet, know that before any practice is to be implemented an inhale and exhale is to be performed before acting. For even further alignment fresh out of resistance, smile after your inhale and exhale. Our children feel us very deeply. Although your intentions are good, they can feel your anger or upset even with an action that is intended to be aligned.

When you start to take on a practice of any kind regarding how you interact with your child, it is imperative that you show yourself a lot of compassion. No matter how simple the practice, it is causing you to expand and with that expansion may come moments of reverting back to conditioning. Sometimes you may feel you have taken three steps forward just to slip up and take one step back. That is never what is happening and your ability to see that is accelerated depending on your ability to love yourself through those moments of reactivity and get right back in the frequency of the version of you that you are becoming.

These practices are causing you to break through conditioned limitations. Once upon a time, your child running up and down the stairs may have taken you over the edge. When you take on a practice that expands you in the way that these practices do, you one day realize that you no longer notice when your child is running up and down the stairs; and when you do realize, you see the beauty in it. You see how awesome it is to have a healthy and able child. You see how blessed you are to have given birth to a child who has such a love for life and enjoys the little things such as going up and down a flight of stairs. The more you expand the more you allow in all areas of your life. It can get a bit overwhelming when we want so much for our lives and have no clue' where to start regarding attaining what we perceive to be more or better than what we currently have. I have found that if we pay attention to how we treat ourselves and the beings that are in our immediate environment and expand in love in those areas, we see that expansion reflected in all the other areas of our lives.

Freedom is what we are talking about experiencing when we put these practices to use with our children. Our children are guiding us to the remembrance of our sovereignty. There is so much freedom in unconditionally loving your child. There are no words to describe the feeling of being with your child and not being worried at all about anything other than the love you are giving to them in the moment and not depending at all on them behaving a certain way in order to remain in that loving place.

Unconditionally loving yourself has to come first. For we are not able to truly love another unless we love ourselves. This is also why breaking and smiling before applying a practice when triggered is key. The self-love is when you take that moment to get yourself together a bit. In doing so, you are able to extend a bit of peace to your child because you gave some peace to yourself. You can only give what you have. When we raise our children and give them the example that we are only at peace and grounded when they are behaving a certain way, then they grow to be dependent on others' states of being to determine their own stability. Our children are either seeing unconditionally loving and sovereign caretakers or they are not. Whatever they are seeing is what they are learning.

YOU ARE THE VISION

You are here to aid in the new paradigm of parenting. You are breaking cycles that have been passed down from generation to generation and it is stopping with you. You, as a child, were only able to physically express your high vibration to the degree that your parents could handle it based on their conditioning. Reacting based on conditioning has been cyclical for generations. That way of parenting is over now for many and the example of those living it continues to send out a ripple across the world, inspiring other parents.

Your child is guiding you to expansion. Anytime you go beyond where you are used to being, there may be a bit of discomfort. You are stepping into the unknown. You do not know what to expect exactly because you have not been there before. If you can learn to appreciate that and look upon it with excitement, it is a whole different ball game. When your child seems to be irritating you it may not seem exciting because you continue to react the same way each time, but I assure you that is an exciting time. For you are being presented yet again with another opportunity to respond in this moment as the parent you prefer, to create your life as a more expanded version than the version of you who is negatively impacted by the behavior of your child. Expansion is always happening no matter what you do, there is no escaping it.

However, you can go at it very slowly or you can accelerate and experience life with your child in a way that you never dreamed possible. How fast do you want to go? The question is not how much you can expand because you are infinity in a body. Your capacity to expand is limitless. The more you expand the more your actions as a human can reflect that expansion and the more your expansion is reflected back to you. How much life do you want to live and enjoy while you are in human form? Your child is guiding you down the fast lane full of tons of love, laughter, abundance, joy, happiness, and so much more.

Your child is guiding you to life as it was lived when you were a child and you did not care about what day of the week it was, and you rarely were ever even aware of time because you were so involved in the moment and never stressed the past or worried about the future. Your child is guiding you to a life both lived totally here in the now and excited about the future because you know your future is a reflection of your willingness to happily expand into more of who you are choosing to become in this moment; and any resistance that arises is not a hindrance to the life your child is guiding you to, but is an invitation for you to step your game up and bring forth even more of you in that moment. Love more. Allow more. Relax more. Trust that all is well. The more you are able to do this with your child the more you can do it with your partner, mother, coworkers, anyone, and everyone - until you realize one day that the very same love that is oozing from your being towards your child is also enveloping every other being you interact with. The more you expand in relationship with your child, the more you expand in all areas and the more abundance you can handle because there is now space for it where there was once resistance and limitation. The more you expand in relationship with your child, the deeper your marriage gets because you have more space for your partner to be more of who they are, where at one time there was resistance and limitation. The more you expand the more your child has space to expand.

This next generation needs that space, because that is how they are going to be able to cultivate the gifts that they brought here to the planet. Our children are the future and the only way they are going to be able to do for the world what they came here to do is if they are not conditioned the way children have been conditioned generation after generation with only a few getting through the cracks and being seen for the geniuses that they are. That time is over. Infinite intelligence wants to come through your child and it also wants to come through you. You choosing to rise beyond your own conditioning allows the space for your child to express the infinite intelligence they came here to express. Your child is your guide but, make no mistake, this is a divine co-creation.

You are reading this not by coincidence but because you too are ready to see change in the world and are willing to be the change that you want to see. We are ushering in a new paradigm of parenting. Parenting response-ably and not re-actively. A way of parenting that benefits children of all ages and truly is not just a way of parenting but a way of being that, if practiced with our children, benefits all.

The challenges you encounter with your children is where the magic happens. We are done experiencing the same triggering moments with our children repeatedly. Your child came here to play, thrive, and create. Not only as children, but for the entire time that they are on this planet. So did you. The relationship between you and your children, if seen and used as the constant feedback system that it is, can clear energetic blockages, provide healing, and amplify the love between you and your children.

It may seem like we have multiple things to do, multiple roles, jobs, etc., but we really only have one job, so to speak. Our alignment. Our children are the best accountability partners. Giving us opportunity after opportunity to expand and always holding us in unconditional love, whether we align or not. If we pay attention to their cues and are committed to making alignment our primary focus, which is being who we naturally are in each moment with no filter, what we create with our children trumps whatever we currently perceive to be our wildest imaginations.

Can we as parents rise above our own programming from our own childhood and what we have witnessed via society, refrain from imposition, and allow more of the light that our children are to come through uninhibited?

We can and we are.

EMPOWERED PARENT AFFIRMATION

My alignment is not dependent upon my child's behavior. My child and I signed up for this divine bond and she/he is playing her/his role perfectly. With every trigger, may I energetically send out to my child and the planet that which equates conceptually to, "My alignment is steady. Thank you for the option to waver, but I've got us. I love you."

ACKNOWLEDGEMENTS

I would like to thank all those who came before me who were dedicated to my *self* and did not let fear stop them from speaking their truth. I would like to thank my mother for being the strong and perfectly rebellious being she is and for following her own inner guidance in her own way throughout her life, despite what anyone had to say about her decisions. I would like to thank Nayelle, my daughter, for guiding me back to my light and showing me what I am *not,* thus allowing me to anchor in what I am.

ABOUT THE AUTHOR

Michelle is a co-active parent empowerment coach and intuitive who works with parents and those who are desiring to reparent their inner child. Michelle enjoys supporting parents as they realize how safe and beneficial it is to follow their hearts in parenting. Michelle uses the many methods that she co-created with her own child in order to transcend limiting beliefs that continued to perpetuate reactions of anger, rage, irritation, and any other emotional label that is ultimately suffering, teachable courses, meditation practices, one on one inquiry sessions, and more to support those who have a deep thirst and hunger to realize more of who they are at their core and minimize more and more of the patterns they have learned from childhood and society. Michelle enjoys seeing time and time again how the parent/child dynamic is an incubator and accelerator for our realization of the love, compassion, peace, and joy that we all have access to in each moment. Working with Michelle is a co-active partnership and only recommended for those who are excited about stretching beyond their current comfort zones and who feel ready to prioritize peace over everything and who would love to experience how this can be done within the parent/child dynamic.

CONTACT

Website: http://www.yourchildisyourguide.com/

TikTok: https://vm.tiktok.com/TTPdMSnDK4/

Instagram:
https://www.instagram.com/yourchildisyourguide

Podcast: https://podcasts.apple.com/us/podcast/not-broken/id1478518194?i=1000551051571

Podcast:
https://open.spotify.com/episode/4R6xLHjzPj0hGGm99NyYHI?si=0kPhFnoZT7K-iUkXMU2klQ